uddenly Marcia was surrounded by a crowd, screaming angrily and pounding on her car with their hands. Frantically she shifted into reverse, glancing in the rearview mirror to see if she could back off the curb and escape. "I've got to get out of here!" she cried, "Oh Lord, help me get away!"

At that moment a rock crashed through the windshield. A cheer rose from the crowd, and the next instant a bottle flew against the windshield. It broke on impact, splashing gasoline through the gaping hole and into the car. Before Marcia could comprehend what was happening, a stone wrapped in a burning cloth flew through the broken window. Instantly flames shot up inside the car as the gasoline ignited. . . .

THE SOWETO LEGACY

LORRY LUTZ

LIVING BOOKS®
Tyndale House Publishers, Inc.
Wheaton, Illinois

To our children,
NATHAN,
MARK,
RANDY,
SHEILA,
and
RODNEY,
who grew up
in South Africa
knowing
there had to be
a better way

FOREIGN PHRASES

Bantu — the African people
The Dominee — the Dutch Reformed pastor
Goeie more, mevrou — Good morning, madam
Ikhaya — a servant's quarters in the back of white
　　　residences
Kaffir bootjie — nigger lover
Matriculation (Matric) — a government exam at the
　　　end of high school which determines whether
　　　or not a student passes
Nkosikazi — Chief's wife, a term also used in respect
　　　for white married women
Ouma — Granny
Tot siens, mevrou — Good-bye, madam
Yebo — Yes, OK

Front cover photo by D. W. Hamilton/The Image Bank

Living Books is a registered trademark of Tyndale
House Publishers, Inc.

First printing, October 1988

Library of Congress Catalog Card Number 88-50700
ISBN 0-8423-5826-9
Copyright 1988 by Lorry Lutz
Printed in the United States of America

CONTENTS

INTRODUCTION

The word *Soweto* conjures up scenes of dogs lunging at defenseless children, of armored vehicles loaded with boyish-looking white soldiers, of black children throwing rocks, and of screaming crowds dancing and chanting slogans.

But few understand the frustrations, the misunderstandings, the anger and fear that led to the 1976 explosion in Soweto (acronym for the Southwestern Township located outside of Johannesburg) that was splattered across the television screens of the world. Though many of the laws and restrictions have been lifted in the intervening years, much of the underlying bitterness and antagonism remains—and apartheid is still basically intact.

Yet on both sides of the color line in this beautiful country, people long for justice and reconciliation. Tragically, blacks and whites have had little opportunity to see the beauty in each other, to appreciate the special gifts God has given each culture, or to put themselves in each other's shoes.

Having lived in South Africa for twenty-two years, I know there are no easy answers. But after the tragedies of the past ten years, at least there are more people like those you will find in this story, who are beginning to ask the right questions and find a new way to respond.

All of the characters in this story are fictitious. But there are many people in South Africa, both black and white, who can identify with the people and situations portrayed here.

PROLOGUE
The Arrest

There was no warning. One minute Jacob was looking in the window of a men's clothing store, dreaming of buying a pair of wing-tipped Florsheim shoes to replace the plastic thongs on his feet, and the next minute a heavy white hand gripped his shoulder and swung him around.

"Where's your pass, *kaffir?*" the grim-faced policeman demanded.

Jacob stared wordlessly at his thongs, wishing they were wings. He had been warned by his sister not to go into downtown Johannesburg until she found a job for him.

He could hear Thandi saying, "You're in Johannesburg illegally, Jake—it doesn't matter that Mother and I have lived here all our lives. You've been out in the country with Granny for so long that you've lost your right to stay here. The only hope is for me to try to get you a job through some of my white friends. Then you may be able to get a pass. But in the meantime, stay close to home. If the police pick you up without a pass, they'll throw you in jail."

The angry voice broke into his thoughts. "Didn't you hear me, *kaffir?* I asked for your pass."

"I don't have one, boss," Jake mumbled.

"So, you're another one of those natives who thinks he can just come into Johannesburg from the country whenever he wants to. It's fellows like you that hang around on the street, carrying knives and attacking people."

Turning to a second officer who had just joined them, the man nodded and in an instant the two grabbed Jacob and threw him against the wall.

Stunned from the blow of his forehead striking the rough bricks, Jacob could feel their impatient hands frisking his body; the twenty-five cents for his train fare back to Soweto fell out as they pulled his pocket inside out. From the corner of his eye, he saw the coin wobble across the sidewalk and disappear.

Satisfied that Jacob was not carrying a weapon, one of the officers pulled him away from the wall and ordered him to hold out his hands. Instantly the officer fastened a pair of handcuffs on Jacob's wrists, putting them on so tightly that Jacob winced as they were locked. Then the officers shoved Jacob in front of them and directed him to a blue police van parked across the street.

Mortified, Jacob hoped no one he knew would see this shameful parade. But the milling crowd of Africans, hurrying to catch their trains back to the black township of Soweto, some twelve miles out of the city, hardly glanced at the little drama; it was commonplace to them.

The officer opened the back of the van and ordered Jacob to get in, then slammed the doors behind him. Jacob could not stand upright in the aisle that ran between the two benches already filled with other prisoners. Though there was open grillwork running along the top of both sides of the van, the dark metal body had absorbed the sun's rays so that the air was stifling from the crush of many bodies.

But as the men good-naturedly squeezed together to make room for him, Jacob sensed an air of camaraderie among them — as though these men had been through this before — and a little of his terror subsided. Realizing Jacob's bewilderment, a well-dressed middle-aged man sitting next to him asked gently, "Is this your first pass raid, son?"

"Yes, uncle. I don't have a pass."

"Uh-oh. That's not good. They'll probably send you back to where you came from after you're released, unless you have some influential friends who can help you. I have a pass back in my other jacket at home. I forgot to take it along this morning — I was in a hurry to get the train for work. I hope my wife will notice before she starts to worry about me when I don't come home tonight. There's no way to let her know where I am."

Growing more fearful by the minute, Jacob asked anxiously, "What's going to happen to us now?"

"Nothing much anymore today. They'll just throw us into a cell for the night. Then, if we're lucky, we'll be booked in the morning."

"Not tomorrow morning," an elderly man in a greasy mechanic's suit interrupted. "Tomorrow is Saturday and the courts aren't open. We'll be sitting in John Foster Square all weekend."

A jumble of groans, angry shouts, and exasperated exclamations burst out as the others realized their dilemma. Some had lived through the dark cells, cold floors, bed bugs, filthy blankets, insipid food, and harsh treatment before. It was just another part of a system that had degraded and dehumanized them, and they had learned to acquiesce rather than to resist. Resistance always made matters worse.

But to Jacob, who had grown up in the sunshine of Zululand, running free in the hot sandy soil, sitting in the mud brick schoolhouse dreamily listening to the bees drone under the eaves, watching his gentle grandmother bend from the waist to feed twigs into the smoking fire under a three-legged black pot, smelling the tantalizing aromas of cooking meat . . . this was an unbelievable nightmare.

And when the heavy cell door clanged shut, imprisoning him and eleven others in a small airless cell, his stomach knotted in fear.

O N E
The Phone Call

The fall morning was bathed in brilliant sunshine.
Marcia loved this time of year, after most of the
rains were over and before the cold snappy winds
of the high veld winter settled in. Everything was
still green and beautiful now. The browns and
beiges of the winter months when frost killed the
grass and drought stunted new growth bored her.
Ever since she'd spent a winter in Europe she'd had
a special appreciation for South Africa's climate.

Marcia glanced at her reflection in the French
doors as she stepped out on the patio to take advantage of one last morning of warmth. Her white
pantsuit set off her tanned complexion even in
that poor reflection. Constant dieting had paid off,
she noted, as she glanced over her slim, well-
proportioned figure in the reflection. The warmth
of her gray-blue eyes and the ready smile of her full
mouth made her more attractive than her rather
commonplace features would warrant. She wasn't

beautiful. Her friends would describe her as compassionate, outgoing, and fun. But if you asked them the color of her eyes, they couldn't tell you for sure. Now Marcia pushed her chestnut brown hair back impatiently from her forehead.

On this Monday morning something nagged at her usual sense of contentment; an inner dark cloud seemed to hang over her. She didn't have to search the recesses of her mind too long to realize she was worried about Geoff, her eldest son. Something was brewing at the university—there was talk about a student demonstration. And she had reason to believe Geoff was involved. She had tried to talk to him about it over the weekend. In fact, it had been just such a balmy morning when she'd found him having breakfast alone on the patio. . . .

Marcia had been glad that her husband Piet had already gone off for a round of golf with Dirk, his boss; she had been looking for an opportunity to talk with Geoff alone.

Geoff had been drinking his tea and reading the morning paper as she came up to him. He had grinned companionably at Marcia and pulled out a chair for her.

"What are you doing up so early?" he'd said. "You must be exhausted after the garden party last night. I thought you'd sleep the morning away."

"I could say the same for you. You must have gotten in hours after Dad and I went to bed. We were still straightening things up at one o'clock, but I didn't hear you come in. Sally must be quite a special girl."

"Not really, Mom. Actually I dropped her off and then I went over to see Ken Roux, who is also on the student council. We had something to work on for Monday."

Just then Angeline, the maid, had appeared, carrying a tray covered with a crisp white cloth. She'd placed it down in front of Marcia and set out a dainty rose china teapot and a matching cup and saucer. This little set had been Marcia's mother's, and she loved to use it for breakfast whenever she wasn't eating with the family. She always marveled that over the years none of the black servants had even chipped it. Perhaps they loved it as she did.

Marcia had hesitated for a moment before talking with her son, stirring her tea and wondering how to begin.

"Geoff —." She'd said his name slowly, gauging her words carefully. "Geoff, your work with Ken wouldn't have anything to do with that Wits demonstration the men were discussing last night, would it?"

For a moment Geoff hadn't answered, then his piercing blue eyes had looked right back into hers as he said, "What would you say if I said yes?"

"Oh, Geoff, I was afraid of that. Don't you realize how dangerous it is for you to get involved in all this political stuff?"

Geoff just shook his head as if to say, "Not you, too.

"Your dad was hopping mad that you confronted Dirk about his political views last night," Marcia had continued doggedly. "It was a good thing you weren't around after the party. He says you're causing trouble for him at the job, especially now that Dirk is running for parliament."

"Dirk expects everyone to go along with his narrow gauge mind," Geoff had retorted in disgust.

"OK, OK, forget Dirk for a minute. You know how your dad feels about the government's policy — exactly the opposite to the things you're always talking about. He blames it on the fact that you're at an English school like Wits, rather than a good Afrikaans university. Don't you think it would be a good idea to drop all this as long as you're in school and living under your dad's roof?"

"Mom, listen. I'm not intentionally trying to cause trouble for Dad. In fact, I promise you I'll do my best to keep out of trouble and not talk so much about the racial situation here at home. But I simply can't go against my own sense of right and wrong."

The phone had shrilled insistently somewhere in the recesses of the house, but Marcia had ignored it.

"Geoff, promise me one thing, that you won't — "

"Telephone, madam," the maid had called from the doorway.

"Coming, Angeline." Marcia had gotten up from her chair then turned to look down at Geoff. "Promise me you won't get involved in that demonstration at the university on Monday."

"Look, Mom, let's just forget about the demonstration. It might not even take place. With the

there—Angeline has had the same problem." She was hoping to appease her mother-in-law; they'd already hired and fired two other gardeners since she'd come, and Moses did seem like a reliable sort.

Marcia really didn't want to think about servants' problems today. She had other things nagging at her mind. If only she could find out whether or not the students were demonstrating—and if Geoff was involved. The news wouldn't be on the radio until one o'clock midday and television didn't begin until six in the evening, so there was no way of finding out what was going on unless she called Pieter. And that she couldn't do! Suddenly an idea came to her mind, and she jumped up from the table, murmuring, "Scuse, Ouma, I just remembered a phone call I have to make."

Back in the study she shut the door, making sure that no one coming down the passage would overhear her conversation. She dialed and waited as the phone rang three times before her friend Ruth answered. Her voice was breathless, as though she'd been running.

"Oh, hello Marci—I was out in the yard. I'm glad you didn't hang up before I got here."

Marcia always felt a lift when she talked with Ruth. They'd met at a women's luncheon about a year ago and discovered that they were practically neighbors. Since then Ruth had invited Marcia to a Wednesday morning Bible study at her house, and she found herself looking forward to these weekly gatherings with increasing anticipation.

"Sorry I caught you at the wrong time," Marcia began, but Ruth cut her off.

"No, I'm glad you called. In fact, you were next on my list. How did your garden party go on Friday?"

"Oh, the party itself went well. Everyone seemed to enjoy the food and it was a perfect evening to eat outdoors."

"I know, you couldn't have ordered a better one."

"But we did have a bit of a problem."

"I thought you sounded a bit down."

"Geoff upset Pieter—he spoke his piece about how the government treats the Africans."

"Uh-oh—I'll bet that didn't go down well with Pieter."

"Or his boss."

As Marcia explained the incident she could still see the group of men standing around the grill holding paper plates loaded with rich food. . . .

They had looked like an ad for good living in South Africa. Tanned from hours on the golf course or tennis courts, their white shorts or light colored safari suits had showed off muscular thighs and arms.

Pieter Steyn, Marcia's husband, stood taller than the rest of his friends, and the cut of his dark hair reflected his precise and tidy mind. A sense of pride had welled up in Marcia, as it had so many times during their twenty-three years of marriage. She watched him deftly caring for the needs of his guests—turning a steak on the fire for one, signaling for a refilled glass for another, skillfully prodding the discussion so that everyone was included.

To most people Piet appeared strong and decisive, but Marcia knew the sensitive emotions hidden under the confident exterior. And she'd learned to recognize the signs of his quick temper, which he held under steely control most of the time.

No one had been surprised at Piet's quick rise in government circles. He served as a legal consultant to the head of the Department of Internal Affairs. When rumors surfaced that Dirk, his boss, was a possible candidate for parliament, Piet had teased Marcia that he might have to trade her in for an Afrikaans version if they were going to fit into high Nationalist Party circles.

Sometimes she voiced her fear that her English background would hold him back, but then he swiftly reassured her that her loyalty and encouragement were all that was expected of her. She wished he were as generous in judging Geoff.

As Marcia had walked up to join the group around the barbecue, she had noted their serious faces as they hung on Dirk's words.

" . . . and a number of them have approached me about this. I think Bosshof is getting too soft, and they are worried where he'll stand if he's elected to parliament again."

Marcia had groaned inwardly. She hated it when the fellows started talking politics, and yet they never seemed to be able to avoid doing so. The last time the Retiefs had been over they'd sat up until after midnight, the women hiding their bored yawns in their cups of tea while Dirk and Pieter dissected the latest government policies.

Dirk had continued, "Some of the boys are worried about Bosshof's liberal position on his Bantu policy. That's why they want me to run for parliament in this constituency. They think I'll take a tougher stand on maintaining our Bantu policies in the urban areas."

"Hear, hear!" The men had nodded in agreement as Pieter broke in to ask, "How are you going to get Bosshof to step down so you can run?"

"Oh, Kruger and several others in parliament are putting pressure on him. They've threatened to expose his statements publicly. You know he was urging that black housing be put into the hands of the Bantu urban council and that funds be turned over to them to handle as they see fit. Can't you imagine the mess they'd make of it?"

"Ya, like letting a bunch of kids have a free hand in a candy store," chimed in Fred Schuster, who lived just down the street from the Steyns. "Next thing you know he'll want to repeal the Immorality Act so that blacks and whites can sleep together."

Indignantly Pieter had spoken up. "He wouldn't dare speak out for mixed marriages. But he has been pretty open about the housing issue. After we pay the taxes and put up with all the nonsense that goes on out there — policing the place night and day to keep the natives from pouring in here by the millions — he wants us to turn it over to them just like that? He wouldn't dare run again if word of that got out."

"And what's worse," Dirk had added, "old Bosshof is playing footsie with the kids at the university. I hear the student council at Wits has decided to stage a protest about the township's housing situation. They asked Bosshof to come and fill them in on all the details. He was over there last week meeting with them as though they were long-lost buddies. He's just lucky the paper didn't get hold of that. We'd rather have him just step down quietly, but if he refuses, we have a few people who know how to leak to the press what he's been doing."

"And maybe that will just mean Bosshof will get more votes than ever." The young voice had broken across the men's unanimity like a karate chop. "Maybe more people than you think are wising up to the mess the Nats have made of the African situation and are ready to vote for a humanitarian like Van."

Startled, the men had turned to see Geoff, who had slipped up to join the group on his way up from the pool. Even in her shocked anger, Marcia had reveled in her son's bronzed attractiveness. If the cluster of men had resembled an ad for good living, Geoff typified an ad for a rugby superstar. She could almost see his piercing blue eyes fringed in thick lashes staring down from a billboard at an ever-present bevy of female admirers.

Geoff's curly dark hair had been wet from the pool, and he'd had his towel slung around his neck to keep his collar from getting wet. Against his yellow shirt, his skin looked almost as dark as an Indian's — the results of weeks in the summer sun during the university break.

Marcia could remember seeing Dirk's eyes narrow in awareness as he turned around all too quickly to face Geoff. But his voice had been calm as he had challenged, "Just what do you mean by that, young man? The very good life you lead is because we've made sure the blacks won't take it away from you. Why are you kids so determined to throw away what we've worked so long to secure?"

"Sure it's a good life, Mr. Reteif, for you and me and anyone else whose skin is the right color. But a lot of us are sick and tired of riding the backs of other people who can never have what we have. Bosshof may be your generation in age, but he thinks like we do."

Pieter had thrown an angry glance at Geoff as he warned, "Mind your manners, Son. You know better than this."

"Let him talk," Dirk had countered expansively as if welcoming another opinion. "It's a free country, you know." But no one had laughed as Dirk intended. In fact, tensions seemed to be mounting.

Embarrassed and furious with Geoff for his insolence, Pieter had not argued with Dirk. He simply stood there looking at the ground, and Marcia had known he was hoping Geoff would be quiet.

"Like I said, Mr. Reteif," Geoff had gone on calmly, "we've been riding the blacks long enough—"

"Riding them?" interrupted Dirk. "Have you ever been in the rest of Africa where the blacks have all the say? Most of those countries are on the verge of bankruptcy; the only thing that keeps them going is the dole from the West. Our blacks have the highest standard of living anywhere on the continent.

"Ya, and better housing, too," chimed in Fred. "You should see the shanties the blacks live in on the outskirts of Nairobi. We don't have anything like that in Johannesburg."

But Geoff wouldn't back down. "At least in those countries the African is free to own his own land—wherever he can afford to buy it. Here all the land in Soweto belongs to the government. Blacks have no sense of security right here in the city where many of them were born and grew up. You can't tell me that's fair. It's time we gave them the same breaks that—"

"Geoff," Marcia had cut in lightly, moving into the fray, picking up empty glasses. "You sound just like all these stuffy old men who are always getting involved in politics." Then she'd noticed Sally Hewitt, Geoff's current favorite, emerging from the house looking fresh and beautiful after her swim. "Why don't you and Sally get the food organized for the rest of the young people?" she'd coaxed with a smile. "They must be starving after all that exercise." And she had reached out to give him a little shove.

As if suddenly remembering his duty to his guests, Geoff had said, "Excuse me, Mr. Reteif. Guess we'll finish this conversation some other time."

Now, as Marcia recounted the confrontation, she sensed Ruth's warm understanding even over the phone. "I was relieved that I finally got Geoff to look after his friends. But you can imagine that

Piet was furious. I've spent the weekend dreading a scene between them. Fortunately Goeff's been gone most of the weekend — studying I suppose — and Pieter took me out yesterday. So we've avoided a blowup so far."

"I am sorry, Marcia. I'm sure Piet didn't appreciate Geoff speaking up in front of his boss. But maybe they needed to hear the other side."

Marcia sighed. "I just hope it doesn't go further than talk, Ruth. That's why I called. I'm really worried." She glanced at the door to make sure she'd closed it tightly, then went on. "Pieter doesn't know this of course, but Geoff is involved some way in those Wits demonstrations planned for today. It has something to do with the housing policy out in Soweto."

"Oh, what demonstrations?"

"I don't really understand what it's all about, though some of the things Geoff has talked about seem to make sense. But I know there'll be trouble with the police if the students demonstrate. And that's what's got me worried. You—you haven't heard anything about it have you?"

Ruth's warm voice evidenced her concern for her friend. "No, I haven't, Marci. Tell you what, I'll call Jim. He works right down on Commissioner Street, and if there's anything happening down there, he would know."

"Would you, Ruth?" Marcia replied, relieved that Ruth had anticipated her request. She had been sure Ruth's husband would know if anything was happening.

"I may not get through to him right away," Ruth went on, "since he had a meeting scheduled with the head of the firm this morning. So don't worry if you don't hear from me for awhile."

"Oh, I don't want you to bother Jim if he's busy. Maybe you should just forget about it. I'm probably worrying for nothing anyway."

"It's no trouble, Marci. I usually call Jim once during the day anyway, and if he's busy, his secretary just gives him the message. I'll call you back after I've talked with him."

For a while Marcia busied herself in the study so she'd be near the phone when Ruth called back. *I'm like a love-bitten teenager waiting for her heartthrob to call*, she thought. *I may as well go and start Angeline on lunch*. Then, as she opened the study door, she heard voices in the kitchen— Ouma was talking angrily with someone.

Marcia entered the kitchen where she saw Moses standing at the kitchen door, a sullen, angry look on his broad face. He wore the threadbare navy jacket he usually wore to and from work on the train, and that he hung on a hook in the garage while he worked.

He didn't say a word as Ouma berated him, "First you spend three hours doing a job that should have taken you thirty minutes, then you disappear for an hour. Now you tell me you don't feel well and have to go home. Well, you don't have to bother coming back. I don't need a lazy kaffir who can't be depended on. You're all alike—you complain about poor pay and mistreatment, but you can't put in an honest day's work. You should be ashamed of yourself, boy."

Marcia wanted to intervene; Moses certainly didn't look very well. But the garden was Ouma's responsibility, and if she didn't want to keep Moses on, that was her business.

Ouma reached into her pocket and pulled out several rand notes. "This is for what you didn't do today. I shouldn't really pay you at all."

Moses stuffed the notes in his pocket, his eyes flickering across Ouma's face with a mixture of anger and desperation. From his inside jacket pocket he pulled out a well-worn green booklet, its corners bent and frayed from much use. Without a word he handed it to Ouma, flipping the page open with his dirt encrusted finger.

"Oh yes, you'll want me to sign you off so you can get a job somewhere else," remarked Ouma as she picked up a pen from the counter. "Let this be a lesson to you, boy. The next time you work for someone, work hard. I've taught you a lot of things about gardening. If you would just put in a day's work, you could make a good gardener."

"Yes, madam," was all Moses mumbled as he turned and walked down the driveway to the road, his shoulders sagging as if his plastic bag was filled with steel weights instead of a tattered blue checkered shirt.

Marcia groaned inwardly. She'd be listening to Ouma's recitals of her woes with the gardener for the rest of the day, and they'd have to go through the whole ritual of hiring a new one again. Sometimes she wished she had the nerve to tell her mother-in-law that if she'd offer a gardener a living wage, he might give her a day's work. But the old lady was already shocked at having to pay as much for a day's work here in the city as she had given in cash to a farm laborer for a month. She didn't comprehend that a man couldn't feed his family, let alone send his children to school, on what she was willing to pay.

I'll be sounding like Geoff if I'm not careful, Marcia thought as she busied herself with pulling some leftovers out of the fridge for Angeline to fix for lunch. She hardly heard Ouma's complaining recital as the heavy weight of her own concerns pushed down upon her again. It was an hour since she'd talked with Ruth. Should she call her again to find out if she'd gotten through?

Suddenly, as if to answer her question, the telephone broke into Ouma's soliloquy and Marcia excused herself, bypassing the phone in the hall to take the call behind the closed door of the study.

"Hello Ruth," she answered breathlessly as she sank into the chair near the phone. "I've been — "

"Mother? Mother, this is Geoff."

"Geoff? Oh, I'm so glad you called. I thought you were Ruth, returning my call." Her anxiety spilled out into her voice as she urged, "Everything is all right, isn't it Geoff?"

In the moment's hesitation before Geoff responded, Marcia could hear men talking in the background. Then she heard him say in a strained voice, "Mother, I'm being held by the police at

John Foster Square. I can't talk now, but could you please come down here right away. I can't hold up the phone — just ask for me at the main desk." And he was gone, leaving Marcia grasping the receiver so tightly a spasm of pain shot down her arm and fear short-circuited her breath.

T W O
The Request

Marcia stood in the slow moving line which led to the officers' desks. There two boyish looking officers with short regulation haircuts politely answered questions and filled out endless papers. News of the Wits demonstration and the ensuing police intervention had spread quickly, and the room was crowded with worried parents who had come to try to release their children on bail.

To Marcia, the last hour was a befuddled dream. She had lied to Ouma, telling her Ruth had invited her for a spur-of-the-moment lunch and hoping Ouma wouldn't ask why she took the car when Ruth only lived a little over a block away. Thankfully the late morning traffic from Bryanston into Johannesburg was light, but even at that it took her almost a half hour to find a parking place near the central police station in the downtown district.

It was almost a relief when she walked into the large sterile reception area and saw other parents looking just as distraught as she felt. There were men in dark business suits who were tense and ill at ease, while several women dabbed at their eyes and tried to compose themselves.

An air of disbelief hung over the room. These were obviously upper middle class families whose children had come through South Africa's school system with high matriculation passes, distinctions, and honors. Otherwise they would never have been accepted into the prestigious and highly selective Witswatersrand University.

Marcia took her place at the end of one of the lines. The man in front of Marcia turned to speak to her. "Your son involved in this mess, too?"

"I—I guess so. I don't know much about it. He just called me to come and get him. Do you know what happened?"

Several other parents had gathered closer, a common unity breaking down any barriers.

"All I know," interjected a distinguished looking gray-haired man who might have been a lawyer, "is that the students were marching from Wits toward downtown carrying banners about lack of housing rights in Soweto. Some kids drove by in a car, jumped out, and shouted insults like *"Kaffir bootjie"* at them. I guess someone picked up a stone—no one knows who—and before you know it, there was a fight.

"The police, of course, were right on the spot. The students were demonstrating illegally, so they were asking for trouble from the beginning."

"But the police didn't have to beat them with their clubs! They're only youngsters," complained a mother, breaking into tears again.

An irate father exploded, "The dumb kids got what they asked for. I warned my son not to get involved in this business. The government knows what it's doing. Those blacks aren't going to thank him for ending up in jail and probably getting kicked out of school just for them."

"Oh, do you think that will happen?" someone asked, and there was a crescendo of concern as parents considered this even greater threat.

Seeing Marcia's anguished look, the man in front of her patted her arm and tried to reassure her. "Don't worry. I don't think they'll get more than a warning. After all, this is the first time they've done anything like this. The fact that the police are letting them out without a hearing is an encouraging sign."

"Are you sure?" Marcia asked, feeling the first spark of hope since Geoff's phone call.

"Yes, that's what I've been told. Ordinarily they wouldn't get out until they appeared before the magistrate. They may have to come back to court in a week or two to face the judge, but my guess is he'll give them a suspended sentence." Then he sighed, "Unless, of course, there's more to this than meets the eye."

Before Marcia could answer, the clean-shaven, adolescent looking constable called, "Next," and her newfound friend moved up to the counter.

Where will this all end? Marcia pondered nervously. *Is Geoff involved in something sinister or*

dangerous just to stand up for the rights of blacks!
As far as she was concerned, they'd always treated
the blacks who worked for them well — except of
course for the fact that Ouma didn't want to pay
them very much. But Marcia had never thought
about what it would be like to live as the blacks
did in South Africa. She thought they always
seemed so cheerful, singing and talking animatedly to their friends as they walked down the
street. And she'd never really seen a starving African. They just had, well, their place.

But now she was in one of their places. This
stark, cold, threatening room somehow brought
to mind the story of Kumalo in Alan Paton's novel,
Cry the Beloved Country, which every South African school child had to read. She remembered crying when the old pastor from the country found
his son in the prison in Johannesburg, accused of
killing a white man.

The heavy sorrow of that father had been so
vivid — a man in pain and anguish over his beloved
child — the same kind of anguish she felt pouring
over her now.

Until Goeff's disquieting views provoked those
uncomfortable family discussions, it had been a
long time since Marcia had allowed herself to
think about the blacks as people with deeply felt
emotions and heartbreaking problems. To her
they had always been kind of adolescent. Her
mother used to tell her that she must "be kind to
the natives" because they were more like children — children who needed to be taken care of.

Marcia had more or less accepted that idea

without giving it much thought. She'd trained her own children to be respectful to the blacks who worked for them. Sometimes when they told uncomplimentary stories they'd heard at school about blacks, she realized there were other influences on their formative minds that she couldn't control. One time she recalled that a native had been hit by a car just down the street, and the ambulance that answered the call for help refused to take him to the hospital because it was for whites only. She'd heard Geoff and his school chums discussing this.

"You wouldn't want them to use the same oxygen mask on your face that they had used on some kaffir, would you?" she heard the neighbor boy ask. "My mother says they are dirty and spread disease. That's why we have to have separate ambulances."

"Ya, and besides, they stink," Geoff had replied.

That time Marcia had intervened, severely reprimanding the boys for such uncharitable observations.

But Geoff had become more politically conscious after he started attending Wits. More and more he argued for fairness and rights for blacks, antagonizing Pieter and upsetting Ouma. Marcia wasn't sure where Geoff got his new ideas, or even how deeply committed to them he'd become. Last Friday's confrontation at the party had been bad enough. But her heart turned to ice when she thought of Pieter's reaction to Geoff's arrest!

Filling in the forms and answering questions was far less painful than Marcia had expected. The young constable treated her kindly, as though he sensed her embarrassment. Now as she waited for Geoff to emerge from the door that led to the cells, her apprehension grew. A few of the young people had come out with bruised faces, and one young man wore a blood-stained bandage around his head. Geoff had sounded all right on the phone, so at least he hadn't been seriously hurt; an injury would be just one more thing to explain to Pieter.

After what seemed an endless wait, a sober looking Geoff was ushered into the reception area by a policeman no older than he. Geoff looked disheveled—his shirt was smeared with dirt and the sleeve was half torn off—but he seemed unharmed.

"Thank God," Marcia cried involuntarily as she threw her arms around him and, against all her determined resolve, burst into tears.

"I warned you not to get involved in this Geoff," she wailed as he gently led her through the crowd.

"I know, Mom. I'm sorry you had to come down here and go through this. But I didn't know who else to call. I don't dare let Dad know."

"Oh, he'll find out, Geoff. You know he will." Marcia dabbed at her eyes, unwilling for curious passerby to see her upset. "It will be all over the papers tonight. Oh, Geoff, you are a fool!"

As Marcia unlocked the car door, Geoff glanced at his watch. "Could you drop me off at Wits, Mom? I could make my last class and save something of this day."

"Looking like that?" Marcia queried as she rolled down the window. "Shouldn't you come home with me and get changed before your father gets home from work? How are you going to explain that torn shirt?"

"Oh, I'll still get home before he does. But, Mom . . . , Geoff hesitated, his young face looking grim. "I've got another favor to ask of you. There's someone else who's going to be in a lot more trouble than I am unless I can warn her."

"We were not in this demonstration alone today," Geoff went on, avoiding Marcia's troubled gaze. "A group of us have been working at the African Family Commission. You know, helping black families with legal problems, housing needs, things like that. You just don't know what families put up with in Soweto, Mom. There are thousands on the list for housing; young couples have to live with their families for years in tiny, overcrowded conditions before they can get a house of their own."

"But Dirk was just telling us about all the new units going up out there every month," interjected Marcia.

"Sure, there are some new four-room houses going up, but it's simply not enough and not fast enough. But there are worse things, like men working in Johannesburg for years while their families have to stay in the country because they can't get permits for them to come to the city. And widows being put out when the breadwinner dies. That's what we've been trying to change. We believe families should be able to live together."

Geoff's voice became more urgent as he turned in the seat to face her. "We have been planning for months to demonstrate for changes in the pass laws. Today was just the first . . . you've got to promise me not to breathe a word of this to anyone. I shouldn't be telling you these things, but I need your help."

Marcia stared at Geoff, wanting to cover her ears so she could blot out his words. But he continued in a grim voice.

"There's a girl who has kept all our minutes—lists of people assigned to certain jobs, letters, everything we've planned. She always took these home with her—we were afraid the police might raid the offices of the Family Commission. But now she's in danger."

Geoff glanced over his shoulder as though fearing he might be overheard. "From the way the police were questioning us, I'm sure they are on to some of our other plans."

Seeing Marcia's horrified expression, Geoff tried to reassure her. "We weren't going to become terrorists, Mom. We just wanted to bring these awful conditions out in the open. Why, this girl Thandi told me about her brother Jacob. He came back to live with them a few weeks ago after he finished school in the country where he'd stayed with his granny. Thandi's mother is sick and can't work regularly anymore, so Jacob wants to take care of her. But Thandi is scared to death he'll get picked up by the police for not having a pass. Don't you see? People should know things like this are going on!"

"I'm sure the authorities are aware of these situations, Geoff. They just can't let in every black who wants to come into Johannesburg. We've got enough unemployment and crime in the city right now."

"Please, Mom, don't take Dirk Retief's line. Those Nats have everyone bamboozled into believing this is the right way for South Africa."

Geoff leaned over to put his hand on Marcia's shoulder. "There isn't time now to go into a long discussion, Mom, but I need your help. Thandi must be warned to destroy all the minutes, and especially the plans with the lists of names and responsibilities—not only for her sake, but for mine. I'm sure the police will connect today's demonstration with the African Family Commission. And if they do, they'll be out to Thandi's place tonight to raid her house. I don't dare go to Soweto, not after being arrested today. But—"

"You're not asking me to go out to Soweto, Geoff?"

"It wouldn't take you more than an hour, Mom. You could be back long before Dad gets home. All you have to do is tell Thandi she must destroy all the papers."

"But Geoff, I've never been out in the township before. Even if I knew where to go, I don't have a permit. You know it's illegal for a European to go out there without one. I could be arrested myself!"

"Some people go out there all the time without a permit. Women take their cleaning ladies home; businessmen go out. I've seen them."

"You go out there?"

"I've only been out there twice, and I don't like it. It's just dirt roads and cement block houses. It depresses me. But both times I've gone out, no one has stopped me for my permit. I'm pretty sure you'd have no problem in the middle of the day."

Marcia sank back into the driver's seat and closed her eyes.

"Oh, Geoff, I can't do this. It's illegal, it's unsafe, and . . . what would I tell your dad?"

"Please, Mom. Just think of the consequences if you don't go. It could mean jail for Thandi and everyone else involved in the plan." Geoff reached over and took her limp hand in his own. "I wouldn't ask you to do it if there were any danger. But Soweto is quiet — as quiet as our own neighborhood in the middle of the afternoon. Everyone is at work in Johannesburg; there are mostly children on the streets . . . and Dad will never have to know."

"What makes you think they are going to raid Thandi's house?"

"I'm almost positive. Several of us were questioned about our contacts with the Commission, and those blokes don't leave a stone unturned."

"And your name is on those lists?"

Geoff nodded. "Mine, and the names of a lot of other committee people who are just trying to help make life easier for black families."

The silence hung between them as Marcia turned her head and stared, unseeing, out the window. Then with a sigh she turned the key and pulled slowly into the street.

"OK, Geoff," she heard herself say, "where does Thandi live?"

T H R E E
The Visit

Marcia clutched Geoff's hastily scribbled directions in her hand, watching for the turnoff to Soweto.

"You'd better go through Johannesburg and out Main Reef Road," he told her. "That way you'll come into Soweto in Dobsonville where Thandi lives, and you won't have to drive for miles through the township. It's a little farther that way, but you'll be less likely to get lost."

The two-lane road wound past the West Rand gold dumps, their once golden shimmering beauty now covered with pampas grass and other hardy high veld shrubs.

So far no one had paid any attention to her. Thankfully there wasn't much traffic on the road, but she knew by late afternoon it would be a mass of buses, trucks, and taxis as thousands of blacks returned home from work in Johannesburg and other white suburbs. Geoff had told her this was the only road leading into Soweto from the northwest.

That's really strange, thought Marcia as she maneuvered her car on the narrow curve. *I wonder why they haven't built more roads?* It dawned on her that she had been skirting Soweto for a number of miles without any other access.

Geoff had described a "buffer zone," about a mile or two of fields, mine land, and wasted area. As she crested the hill, she saw the township spread before her as far as her eye could see. The valley below was filled with rows and rows of houses that disappeared over the hills to the right and left. A gray haze still hung over the valley, a remnant of the countless fires in countless stoves.

"Why, it's massive," she breathed. "It's like another city, tucked away beyond the hills — one I've never seen before!"

As Marcia neared the edge of the township, the palms of her hands were wet with perspiration. She clutched the wheel rigidly, and a feeling of terror mounted as she entered the forbidden area.

Just then a child darted across the street, and Marcia slammed on her brakes and her wheels screeched.

Slow down there girl, she thought to herself. *No point in attracting unnecessary attention.*

She glanced around and saw that it was just as Geoff had said — the streets were fairly empty of people except for old women selling mealies cooked over hot braziers and school children in their uniforms and bare feet strolling along amiably with their friends. She'd read about the "double streaming" in Soweto schools. *These kids must be the morning stream going home*, she thought.

There seemed to be no malice in their expressions nor surprise that a white woman was driving out here alone. In fact, some of the smaller children waved and grinned, calling "Good morning, missus," practicing their few words of English on her.

The houses were monotonous, all the same size and style. And some enterprising official must have had a sense of humor, for they were painted in faded pinks and blues and greens and yellows; tiny little matchboxes surrounded by equally tiny yards. Some of the yards were neat and green with flowers bravely growing along the fence; others were barren and cluttered.

Marcia slowed down the car to watch for the landmark Geoff had written down, the Mountain View Dry Cleaners. He had said the building was painted a bright blue and had a weather-beaten red and white sign over the doorway. She came to the end of the paved road, and her car bounced over the corrugated dirt road. A broken tap was running full blast on the top of a spigot at the edge of the road, and rivulets of mud floated along, carrying boats of withered leaves and crumpled paper. An overturned garbage can spilled its contents onto the road, and she swerved to avoid hitting the refuse. A skinny, bone-outlined dog darted out of the way, its tail hooked between its legs. As she watched it she remembered reading about packs of dogs that roamed the township streets at night, scrounging in the garbage.

Then Marcia's eyes were attracted to a group of children playing along the road. An older girl was dancing with abandon, surrounded by half a dozen youngsters singing at the top of their voices and clapping in rhythm.

Leaning against the building, somberly watching the excitement, was a girl in a faded red plaid dress. The girl reminded her of someone she'd known — the way she rubbed one bare foot against the other. Marcia frowned slightly. She hadn't thought of Busi in years.

It was a long long time ago, and yet it seemed like yesterday. She could still see Busi standing at the back fence of Grandma Mulder's yard. Busi had been living in the servant's quarters with her mother, who was a servant in the house. As a little girl, Marcia used to look forward to going to Grandma Mulder's so she could play with Busi.

Busi had an old doll Marcia's grandmother had given her from the used toy barrel at the church. Marcia and Busi would tie their dolls on their backs like the African women did and pretend to "cook" in a battered pot over a make-believe fire.

Sometimes they would race carrying bottles on their heads. Busi ran almost like a bird along the ground, the bottle standing upright on her head, without using her hands to balance it. But Marcia could never quite manage, and Busi had generously permitted her to use one hand to steady the bottle.

Marcia could still remember the day of her sixth

birthday party. Her grandmother had invited eight little girls who had come in their prettiest dresses carrying surprises wrapped in tantalizing camouflages. Marcia had peeked into the dining room to see the beautiful cake decorated with candy roses, the brightly colored "crackers" that popped when you pulled the ends and were filled with paper hats and prizes.

As she and the other girls had played games out in the backyard, Marcia remembered noticing Busi standing at the door of her room peeking out. She had a clean dress on and was looking wistfully at the laughing girls in their frills and shiny patent shoes. Marcia had run over and grabbed Busi by the hand.

"Come play with us, Busi, we're going to race now. You can show the girls how to run with a bottle on their heads."

But Busi had pulled back, shaking her head. "No," she mumbled, embarrassed, "I don't have any shoes, Marcia. All those girls have shoes."

"Oh, we can take ours off, Busi. Then the race will be fair. Come on, it's more fun to race barefoot anyway."

Gingerly Busi had moved out of the doorway and Marcia pulled her into the circle of girls. In a moment nine blonde heads were bent over nine pairs of black patent shoes as they stripped them off and threw them down on the grass.

Marcia had been the first one up, balancing her bottle on her head, trying to show how well she could race without using her hands. Busi had giggled as she saw the other girls try to walk with the bottle on their heads, and she called instructions. "Pull your chin in. Hold your shoulders back."

Then, suddenly, everything had stopped. Marcia had looked up to see her grandmother angrily looking at her. "Marcia, what is this? Why do you all have your shoes off?" And then she had spotted Busi and added sternly, "Go back to your room, Busi."

Shamefacedly, the other girls had scrambled into their shoes, chatting among themselves to cover up the embarrassed silence. But Marcia had watched Busi run back to the door of the servant's room and stand there awkwardly, rubbing one bare foot against the other.

Now this girl in the red plaid dress was standing there, just like Busi had, rubbing her foot in the same way, standing outside of life and play and things that mattered. *This place must be full of Busis standing on the outside looking in*, Marcia thought to herself. *That must be the way all these people out here feel every time they come into our area.*

As she turned onto a side street Marcia glanced into the rearview mirror and noticed a blue van turning onto the street behind her. Hadn't she seen that same car behind her as she came into Soweto? Could it be following her?

Ignoring Geoff's carefully drawn instructions, Marcia turned left onto the first side street she reached, trying to avoid the deep ruts as she accelerated. She watched with foreboding in her rearview mirror as the blue van turned onto the same road. Then she breathed a sigh of relief when she saw it stop in front of one of the cracker-box houses to let out a passenger.

But Marcia's relief was short-lived, for now there were no recognizable landmarks. Every street looked the same. As she tried to get back on the road she'd left, her car twisted and turned over the corrugated roads, seemingly taking her ever farther from her destination.

Even in her confusion, Marcia was overwhelmed with the monotony of the township and the fact that there seemed to be only the most basic of conveniences. At the back of each house was an outhouse built to service four families. Marcia could see a woman filling a basin at the tap at the side of the toilet—a sign that there was no running water inside the houses. The overhanging wires outside indicated there was electricity, at least in this part of the township.

Marcia was about to stop and ask some of the children where house number 1553 was when she found herself back on the road she'd turned off of so precipitously a few minutes earlier. There were the landmarks Geoff had given her: the cement block church with the red trim on the windows and the soccer field on the left. "Well, sort of a soccer field," he'd explained. "It's a big barren stretch of field with some goalposts stuck into the ground at either end. But they sure play some soccer there. Our Springboks would take the World Cup if they let some of our top black players onto the team—but don't get me onto that. Turn after the soccer field and the fourth house on the right-hand side is the Ngubanes' place."

When she reached the house, Marcia parked her blue Escort in front of the gate, carefully locking all the doors and making sure the windows were rolled up tightly. Even before she opened the door, a dozen children had gathered around, plastering their noses against the windows, flashing their big-toothed grins and chanting in a sing-song fashion, "Good morning, missus."

She held her handbag close under her arm as the children pushed each other for a better position, moving back only to allow her to get out of the car.

She smiled at one little girl who was jostling her baby brother on her back. Suddenly he began screaming with terror when he saw the white woman, and the rest of the children broke into hilarious laughter at his reaction. Feeling somewhat chagrined at his response, Marcia pushed open the gate to the Ngubanes' house and walked up a pathway that was flanked by patches of struggling petunias.

She felt rather than saw that she was being watched from behind the curtained window, but she had to knock two or three times and was almost ready to give up before the door opened.

Standing inside, her expression guarded and suspicious, was one of the most beautiful African girls Marcia had ever seen. *She's just about Geoff's age*, she thought with a pang. The girl's smooth, light brown complexion was the color of coffee with a touch of cream. Her straight, almost European looking nose set off her deepset, ebony eyes, which were fringed with long full lashes. Her full mouth was balanced by rounded high cheekbones, and she wore her hair in the pattern of intricate glistening braids that was so popular with young black women once they left school.

"Hello," Marcia said, breaking the ice. "I'm looking for Thandi Ngubane. I have a message for her from Geoffrey Steyn. Is this the right house?" The girl's impassive face registered no response. She simply nodded her head and motioned for Marcia to step inside. "Good day, madam. Please come in. I'm Thandi Ngubane."

Marcia's eyes swept around the tiny room, taking in the lumpy daybed covered with a heavy "African" blanket. A large wooden sideboard and square dining table filled the room, leaving barely enough space to walk around.

Thandi just watched her silent appraisal, then pointed to a chair. "Please, madam, sit down." As Marcia lowered herself to the edge of the heavy wooden chair, she glanced at a picture of Swaziland's King Sobuza that had been cut out of a magazine and pasted on the rough plaster wall. A plaque bearing the words "Christ is the head of this house" startled her. Why did it surprise her that they were Christians, she wondered.

The shelves of the sideboard were lined with newspaper, the edges cut into scallops. The table was graced by a hand-crocheted, stiffly starched doily on which a vase of brightly colored plastic flowers rested. The concrete floor was partly covered with a worn piece of linoleum. There was no ceiling to cover the exposed rafters and corrugated iron roof. A bare light bulb hung from one of the rafters.

Thandi remained standing, glancing at the closed door which led to the back of the house as she asked guardedly, "What is the message?"

Marcia felt the girl's hostility—and fear. "Thandi, I'm Geoff's mother. He sent me here to warn you." Thandi gripped the back of the chair in front of her as though to brace herself.

"Geoff was involved in the demonstration at the university this morning, and he and some of his classmates were arrested."

"Hau!" Thandi whispered, covering her mouth with her hand.

"I was able to get him out of jail, though he may have to go back for a hearing next week. But he's afraid he's being watched, and that's why he asked me to come and warn you."

Marcia could hear the rattling of a kettle behind the closed door, and automatically her voice dropped, "He thinks the police may come out here to question you. He says you must destroy all the notes and letters. Do you know what he's talking about?"

"Yes," she whispered as she sank down on the cot.

Marcia was astonished to hear herself say, "Shouldn't you go and stay with some of your friends until this is all over?"

Thandi shook her head, "No madam, I'll be all right. Thank you for coming to tell me," and she rose from the couch. Marcia felt she was being dismissed, but somehow she didn't want to go. She couldn't understand her own reactions. It was always hard for her to carry on a conversation with an African, and Thandi wasn't making it easy. She was evidently very intelligent and spoke English well, but kept herself hidden behind that beautiful mask. Still, in spite of herself, Marcia wanted to know more about this attractive girl who carried herself with such dignity.

Then before Marcia could say her farewells, the kitchen door opened, and a woman who seemed to be an expanded replica of Thandi except for the pain etched in her face stood with a tea tray in her hands.

Marcia had heard about the hospitality of Africans but she hadn't thought that they would expect her to drink tea with them. *Well*, she scolded herself, *why not?* Everything was clean and she was thirsty. And didn't Angeline fix her tea for her at home every day? What difference would it make to drink it here?

"Oh, how nice, I've been dying for a cup of tea." Even Marcia could hear the patronizing tone in her voice, but she pushed stubbornly on. "Is this your mother, Thandi?"

Without waiting for a response, Marcia addressed Mrs. Ngubane. "I'm Geoffrey Steyn's mother. I—"

But Thandi quickly interrupted. "Mama, Mrs. Steyn is a friend from the Family Commission. She has come to see if she can help us." Her mute glance at Marcia conveyed desperation. "Mama, I was just going to tell Mrs. Steyn about Jake. Maybe she can help us find him."

Thandi's mother placed the tea cups on the table and began pouring. Just two cups, one for

Marcia and the other for her daughter. And Marcia was startled to see that tears brimmed in Mrs. Ngubane's as she poured the tea. She sat silent as she watched the older woman search unsuccessfully in her apron pocket, presumably for a handkerchief. Then, wiping her eyes with the corner of the apron, she whispered, "Excuse me, madam," and fled into the kitchen leaving Thandi and Marcia looking at each other in consternation.

"What's wrong with your mother?" Marcia asked in concern.

Thandi slumped into her chair and Marcia could see the anger that welled inside her.

"Madam, my brother, Jacob, hasn't been home for four days. We don't know where he is. No one has seen him or heard anything about him. Sick as she is, my mother insisted on going to the hospital and even the morgue yesterday, but there was no trace of him there. We think he's been picked up by the police, but we're afraid to ask questions. Your son would know why I'm afraid, but," she added quickly, "Mother mustn't know anything about that!"

The boy had been gone four days! Marcia remembered the time when Geoff had gotten lost on a hike. They had hunted the veld for him for two hours before they found him and his companions blithely unaware of the furor they had stirred up. But four days . . . four days of imagining the worst and then visiting the morgue to try and find the truth! The nights would be longest, lying there listening to the ticking clock and the dogs foraging in the garbage, hoping for the sound of the creaking gate or a step on the gravel path outside the door. How long the nights would be. No wonder a thought of help pricked Mrs. Ngubane's tension and welled over in a flood of tears.

"Where do you think he is? Maybe I could go and ask about him." Marcia's words poured out before she could stop them. It seemed she was slowly being enmeshed in the Ngubanes' affairs without any choice of her own. Is this what had happened to Geoff, too? Could it be that God was nudging her to get involved?

Thandi responded to Marcia's questions with a little more warmth in her voice. "If he doesn't come home tonight, I'll have someone call the police when I get to work tomorrow. He's probably been picked up for not having a pass. I warned him not to go into the city. You have enough problems on your mind with Geoff, madam. Thank you for offering your help, but I think it's best you don't get involved right now."

Back in her car, Marcia found that an uncomfortable battle raged inside her. All her life she had been a loyal South African. But since she had married into the Steyn family, she had become even more aware of the strong family ties, the deep loyalty to country and law and order, the sincerity and determination to keep this land strong for all its people.

The issues were not simple. Many believed that without the controls and regulations of apartheid, as Dirk Retief had so clearly reiterated, the nation would be bastardized. And the Afrikaaner wouldn't be the only loser. The Zulu, the Suthu, the

Tswana — everyone would lose his or her heritage, culture, and language.

Ouma Steyn used to say, "If we don't keep these natives in their place, everything we've done will be destroyed by people who don't know the first thing about hard work or planning ahead."

Certainly the system has brought prosperity to us, Marcia admitted to herself. Even Americans visiting had remarked about the high standard of living in South Africa. "We can't afford servants and garden boys like you do here," they drawled. "This is really the good life."

But today she'd seen the other side for herself, and she wondered at whose expense she was living the good life. Since she'd been going to Ruth's Bible study, she'd been rethinking many of the values of her life. She'd never realized before that the Bible could impact so many areas of modern life. An uncomfortable sensation disturbed her. Was this yet another area she'd have to reevaluate?

Suddenly Marcia was brought out of her reverie as she crested the hill, for at the bottom of the slope about a quarter of a mile away she could see a police roadblock.

There was no way to turn around without being seen, no side streets to turn onto. A police van stood on each side of the road and four policemen stood on the side, waving the traffic down from both directions.

Ahead of her a truck loaded with men put on its brakes. No doubt the driver was mentally checking his documents: Pass? License and registration in order? Third party insurance disk up to date?

You never knew what they were looking for. Sometimes it was a routine vehicle check; other times it was pass violations or even an escaped criminal.

Marcia had seen such checks on the outskirts of the city, but the police had always waved her on once they saw she was white. Would they do that here? Or would she be arrested for being in Soweto without a pass?

"God help me," she breathed. "Get me past the blockade. Please don't let me be arrested. Pieter would be mortified."

She pulled to a stop behind the truck. The men were already being ordered out, and one of the policemen was checking their passes.

The other came over to her car. He didn't look much older than Geoff, though his immaculate blue uniform gave him a distinct air of authority. His clean-shaven face and short blond hair did nothing to soften the impersonal look in his penetrating eyes.

Marcia rolled the window down, trying to swallow the lump that had risen into her throat, threatening to cut off the air.

"Good afternoon, madam, may I see your permit please?"

Marcia swallowed hard, hoping her fear didn't show. "I—"

"Johan, come here," a voice called, cutting her off.

The young officer turned and ran to help his partner, who was struggling with an African. Marcia watched aghast as the officers struck the man a blow which sent him sprawling. Then the two officers jerked him to his feet and threw him against the van, pulling his arms behind his back. While one held him by the scruff of the neck, the other locked a pair of handcuffs on him.

Barking orders, the officers began thoroughly searching each of the other men from the truck, forcing them to sprawl against the side of the van with their arms outstretched in front of them.

Remembering Marcia who was still waiting in a line which had now grown by three other cars, the officer turned back to her and called, "Lady, you can go on. This will take us some time."

Relieved at the unexpected reprieve, Marcia started her car. She had to restrain herself from putting her foot to the floor to get out of this near disaster. She maneuvered decorously around the blockade, trying not to draw attention to herself. Then breathing a heartfelt prayer of thanksgiving, she headed back for the world she knew.

F O U R
The Threat

Marcia flopped into the kitchen chair waiting for the teakettle to boil.

The experience in Soweto had left her weak and exhausted. It had been a relief to find the house empty when she reached home. Ouma had gone to her weekly women's meeting at the church, and this was Angeline's afternoon off.

Marcia didn't know which had left her most shaken, her visit to the Ngubanes' home or the close encounter with the police. She couldn't erase from her mind the picture of Thandi's mother breaking down over her son's disappearance. She wished she'd never gone out there. She shouldn't have! Geoff had his nerve pushing her into a corner like that.

And it wasn't over yet. She hated to think of Piet's reaction when he found out about Geoff's arrest. Relations between them had been strained for a long time. This would surely be the breaking point—not to mention what it would do to her relationship with Piet if he found out she had deliberately deceived him and had even gone so far as to break the law. *Seeing Geoff in that police station just unhinged me,* she thought. *I would never have agreed to his request if I'd been in my right mind.*

The teakettle whistled shrilly, breaking into her reverie. Marcia automatically poured boiling water into the teapot to heat it, poured it out and added a spoonful of tea and more boiling water. The rich mellow aroma penetrated her consciousness with a soothing effect. She could understand why Pieter usually wanted a cup of hot tea when he walked into the house after a hectic day. It had the hypnotic effect of comfort and habit, like an old pair of slippers.

Suddenly the front door slammed, startling her. "Mom, I'm home!" fourteen-year-old Tim called, and she heard him tramp through the house to his room. She knew he'd soon be out in the kitchen himself for a cup of tea and the sandwiches Angeline had made for the boys before she left at noon.

Sure enough, Tim bounced into the kitchen. Pulling on a soccer jersey, he began rummaging for food as though he'd had nothing to eat all day.

"I'm going to my soccer game, Mom," he said stuffing a double sandwich in his mouth and taking the cup of tea Marcia held out to him. "Gary went right from school. I don't think we'll be home for supper. We're playing a school out in Randfontein, and the game doesn't start until five."

"When do you plan to do your homework?" Marcia asked, knowing that would be Piet's query when the boys didn't show up for supper.

"Oh, we'll be home by eight. Besides, I don't have much tonight. Old Barker was out sick today, so we don't have any math assignment."

Grabbing the last sandwich off the plate, he gave Marcia a quick hug and ran down the hall and out the front door.

Marcia couldn't help smiling at Tim's enthusiasm and single-mindedness. *If only life could always be that simple*, she thought as she tidied up the mess her young tornado had left in his wake.

With Angeline gone, Marcia busied herself in the kitchen getting supper. By the time everyone was home and ready to eat, her spirits had calmed and she could almost put the day's events behind her. She just hoped they could keep the conversation innocuously pleasant at the table.

Ouma had enjoyed her women's meeting. "The Dominee came and spoke to us today. He's a fine man. He asked about you after the meeting, Pieter; he wonders why you don't come to church."

Marcia knew that Pieter had long ago stopped trying to explain to his mother that he saw no need for church in his life. God was all right for an old woman, but Pieter had no time to complicate his busy life with what he called legalistic religious concepts and hypocritical dominees.

But rather than provoke an argument, he mumbled a noncommittal, "Sometime, Ouma, sometime." Then he turned to Marcia to change the conversation. "And how was your day today, honey?" he asked.

Startled out of her own thoughts, Marcia stammered, "Well, I did some things around the house . . . and, oh yes, Angeline was off today, so I fixed supper."

"You went over to Ruth's for lunch, too, don't you remember?" Ouma chimed in.

"Uh, yes, of course, I forgot. I went to Ruth's," she added lamely, a sinking feeling in her heart as she heard herself deliberately lie to her husband.

"I hope you had a quiet, uneventful day, too, Goeffrey," Pieter remarked to his son who had been eating silently, avoiding the conversation that so often ended in frustration and argument. "I saw from the headlines that some of your friends at Wits got themselves into trouble with the police."

Pieter turned to Marcia. "I can't for the life of me figure out why these students waste their efforts and their parents' money getting involved in such things while they're in school."

Turning back to Geoff he asked, "Did you hear any more about the demonstrations at the school today?"

Marcia gently kicked Geoff's leg, hoping to remind him to keep quiet about his part in the incident.

But she saw that Geoff needed no warning. He knew how his father felt about his attitude toward the Africans. They had argued so many times about the rights and wrongs of apartheid, but this was one time Geoff didn't want to be drawn into a discussion that could lead to his exposing his own involvement.

"Ya, sure, Dad, everybody was talking about it. But it was really nothing. A few students got into a brawl with some guys who were baiting them while they walked down the street. The police broke it up in a hurry, I guess."

"I should hope so. Any time our law enforcement officers allow kids to get away with disobedience and rioting like they do in America, our parliament would have something to say about it. What were those students after anyway? I just glanced at the *Star* headlines on my way home."

Marcia threw Geoff a warning glance. "Let's not start talking politics again, Pieter," she said. "Angeline made a delicious pudding before she left this morning. Would you like some now or later?"

The conversation veered away from the dangerous topic, and Marcia didn't even mind hearing Ouma complain about Moses and why she had to fire him. Anything was better than discussing the Wits demonstration and exposing Geoff's part in it.

Suddenly the doorbell rang.

"Who could that be?" Pieter asked. "Are you expecting someone, Geoff?"

Geoff shook his head and started to get out of his chair to answer the door.

"I'll get it; I'm already up," Marcia called over her shoulder as she walked down the hall to the front door.

She pulled it open at the second insistent ring of the bell to find Dirk Retief impatiently standing on the step. Dirk was a big man in every way — big bulky body, big square head, and a shock of steel gray hair which he kept in a short, military cut. He had a broad mouth and a voice to match. His square pudgy hands could have been those of a farmer; they were solid and firm and strong. He often intimidated people when they first met him.

Brought up in the "old school," Dirk was usually gallant and courtly toward women. But the Dirk standing at Marcia's door now was the tough steely administrator who could throw terror into the hearts of those who worked for him — blacks and whites alike.

"Marcia," he began without apologies, "is Pieter here? I've got to talk with him."

"Why, yes, come in. We were just finishing dinner. I'll call him."

Pieter recognized Dirk's voice and was already in the hall to greet him.

"Come in, come in, Dirk. This is a surprise. Come, sit down in the lounge." Then to Marcia, "Get us some tea please, honey."

"This isn't a social call, Pieter," Dirk replied coldly as he followed Pieter into the lounge. "I think you know what I've come to see you about."

"Is there something wrong, Dirk?"

"Wrong? Don't you know what that son of yours has been up to?"

"You mean Geoff?" Seeing Dirk's grim acquiescence Pieter groaned as he threw himself into a chair. "You're going to tell me he was involved in today's demonstrations?"

"Not only involved, Pieter. I have evidence that

he was one of the leaders! The magistrate called me this afternoon to fill me in on all the details. Of course, he didn't know that the father of one of these stupid students was my assistant. He just knew that Van den Berg had put these kids up to this."

"The fool . . . "

Dirk ignored Piet's interruption. "This is the end of him politically. The magistrate let the kids go. He doesn't think it will do the party any good to bring everything out into the open—not until Van is removed from the running. But I couldn't believe it when he told me that Geoff was one of the organizers of the demonstration today."

Dirk leaned his great bulk forward in his chair, pointing his finger at Pieter to add weight to his words. "Let me make this very clear, Pieter. You see to it that your son gets out of this movement immediately—I mean tonight—or I'll have to replace you with someone else in my campaign. The liberals will grasp at anything to undermine our program. What could be more devastating than for them to point out that you, a member of a staunch Afrikaans family and an aide to the upcoming member of parliament, can't convince his own children of the rightness of our cause."

Pieter nodded unwilling agreement. Then he said softly, "I'll call Geoff."

Rising to his feet, Dirk spread his hands in a gesture of refusal. "No, I don't want to waste any more time arguing with Geoff. That's your business. You handle it in your way. I think I've made myself clear." Striding toward the door, he nodded curtly toward Marcia, who stood stricken in the hall. *"Tot siens, mevrou,"* he said and he was out the door before she could respond.

For a moment there was a stunned silence. Ouma, who had been listening unobtrusively in the dining room began weeping softly. Marcia simply stood and stared at Pieter in anguish, the color drained from her face. He sat with his head in his hands, and guilt swept over her as she saw his disappointment and bewilderment. She wanted to put her arms around him and comfort him. In fact she stepped forward to do so when he raised his head and looked at her accusingly.

"You knew this, didn't you? You knew that Geoff was breaking the law by working in a pro-African movement. That's why you're always defending him, trying to keep me from talking about my political views."

"No, Piet, I didn't know. At least not until Saturday . . . ," she faltered. "I sort of stumbled on it by accident, and I tried to stop him. You know how young people are, Pieter. He's idealistic. He doesn't understand what it would mean if the Africans were in power instead of the whites."

"You're damn right he doesn't understand. But as long as he lives in my house, and I pay his school fees, he'll do what I say. I don't know what's happened to you either, Marcia. When you married me, you knew you were marrying into an Afrikaans family. Yet you have always pushed for sending the children to English schools —"

"Are you blaming me for Geoff's involvement?" Marcia interrupted.

"I'm blaming you for letting him go on in this foolishness. Why didn't you tell me when you found out what he was planning? I could have stopped him."

"No, you couldn't."

Marcia and Pieter turned to see Geoff standing in the doorway, where he'd been listening to their conversation.

"Don't blame Mom for my activities, Dad. I'm old enough to make my own decisions. She tried to talk me out of this, but it was my own choice."

Coming over to face his father who had risen to his feet, Geoff continued, "I know you'll never understand why I feel so strongly about the way we treat the Africans in this country, Dad —"

"You don't know what you're talking about," Pieter broke in coldly.

But Geoff continued as though he hadn't even heard his father. "They deserve the same opportunities we have. But look at their lousy school system and the jobs they can't hold because of our laws. We could be the greatest country in the world if we worked together with the Africans instead of alienating them. No, Dad, I'm not an anti-South African — I'm pro. That's why I hate to see us continue with this noose around our necks."

"If you and your communist buddies keep on the way you are, you'll soon have your wish. The blacks will be running this country, enjoying all the good things we built up over the years, and you'll be shining their shoes."

"It doesn't have to be that way, Dad. Don't you see we may still have time to develop trust and cooperation between the races—"

"That's poppycock! And it's not the issue right now either. I'm giving you an ultimatum: either you drop out of the movement or whatever you call it and forget all this *kaffir boetjie* activity, or I stop paying your school fees, and you can leave school and find yourself a job."

Marcia added quietly, "I think your dad means it, Geoff. You'd better not make a foolish decision."

Geoff stood rubbing his toe on a circle on the carpet, as if weighing his words. "This movement, as you call it, Dad, has been put out of business. The police have seen to that. Anything we might have accomplished today was destroyed by the way things turned out. So for the time being you don't have to worry about my jeopardizing your job any further. But I can't promise that I wouldn't take part again if a new opportunity arose."

He started to leave and then turned back and added almost gently, "I'll try not to be an embarrassment to you and Dirk again, Dad, if I can help it. I guess I owe you that much."

"I'll hold you to that," Pieter responded coldly.

Relieved that a crisis had been averted for the moment, Marcia put her hand on Pieter's and Geoff's arms. "Can we call it a truce for tonight?"

Seeing their hesitation, she gave them a gentle shake. "Come on, everything will come out right."

But inside her heart was in turmoil, for she'd suddenly come to the devastating realization that Geoff's position was beginning to make sense.

F I V E
The Appeal

The next few days an uneasy truce settled over the Steyn household. Marcia thought anything would be better than the fierce arguments that cut into her heart like a knife and left the two men she loved eaten up with bitter turmoil.

She wondered if Ouma had felt torn like this when Piet had told her he was going to marry an English girl. Marcia remembered all too clearly their first visit to the family farm in the Free State.

"Don't worry Marcia, they'll learn to love you as I do," Piet had told her as she voiced her fears during the long ride through the golden veld.

"But I can't even speak Afrikaans properly, Piet. And I've never baked a milk tart in my life."

"We've gone all through this before, Marci. Sure my folks wanted me to marry an Afrikaans girl. They even had one picked out for me — one of our neighbors' daughters whose ancestors date back to the Great Trek."

He had put his arm around her and pulled her over closer to him as he said teasingly, "She would have made a nice fat Boer housewife."

"Oh Piet, be serious. You've disappointed your parents, just like your brother did."

"But they got over it and now they love Jacobus' wife like a daughter. Maybe you can't bake milk tarts, but you're a schoolteacher and that should give you points. The schoolmaster is one of the most respected people in the community here."

And Ouma had certainly tried to make her feel welcome. Marcia could still see her standing at the kitchen door when they arrived. She carried her generous figure erect, a picture of strength. Her gray eyes were sharp and penetrating under heavy dark brows and her clear, unlined skin exuded health.

She had opened her arms to them both and welcomed Marcia in broken English, leading her through the large sun-filled kitchen past the scullery where the servant girls were washing dishes in a cheerful atmosphere of domesticity.

Marcia remembered noticing the rows of preserves on the shelves above the sink. Piet had told her how his mother had won blue ribbons at the fair for some of them. Her heart had sunk as she thought of trying to keep up.

But Ouma had done her best to make Marcia feel welcome, giving her the large guest room at the top of the stairs that looked out over the fields of ripening grain. The huge four poster bed was covered with an intricately designed patchwork quilt — another one of Ouma's blue ribbon winners.

The farm house had recently had indoor plumbing added and Ouma had pointed out the bedroom-sized bathroom at the end of the hall. "We made the smallest room into the bath since Pa and I are here alone now. We don't need all the bedrooms anymore," she explained.

Marcia recalled how the tenseness had poured out of her as she soaked in the hot bath, washing away the dirt that had accumulated over the day's drive. She's actually felt herself drifting off to sleep in the soothing waters. Ouma had told her dinner wouldn't be served until seven, when Pa came in from the fields. "So you just have a good rest."

Suddenly the sound of voices had startled her awake. The kitchen was just below the bathroom, and the voices carried clearly through the pipes. Even though they were speaking in Afrikaans, Marcia heard and understood every word.

"But Pa, you haven't even met her — how can you be so sure it won't work?" Marcia recognized Piet's pleading voice.

"Mixing blood never works. The Holy Bible tells us that."

"But Pa, she's a European, like you and me. It's not mixing blood."

"She not of our nation. And you'll turn away just like Jacobus, forgetting your heritage and the suffering of our people until your children won't even speak our language."

"She can speak Afrikaans, and she'll improve.

We can send our children to Afrikaans schools."

"But you won't be a true Afrikaaner anymore.

"Pa, I'll be just as much an Afrikaaner as ever. I work for the government and almost everyone in my office is Afrikaans. I can do more to keep the purity of our nation there than you can here. . . . "

The voices had faded as the men moved to another room. Ouma hadn't said a word, but Marcia could imagine her troubled face as she saw the two men she loved disagree. Marcia had sat rigid in the water, as if it had turned to ice. When she finally got out of the water to get ready for dinner, she was chilled to the bone.

Pieter's father had been courteous but aloof at dinner, while Ouma had tried to bridge the silences with conversation that included Marcia. After Ouma's first question, phrased in awkward English, Marcia urged her to use Afrikaans, *"Ek kan verstaan* [I can understand]," she explained.

Even during the traditional prayers after the meal, when Ouma had called the servants in to sit around on the floor while Pa read out of the big family Bible, Marcia had felt there was only a truce.

And now the cold truce between Piet and Geoff was no easier to live with than the open confrontation. Piet worked long hours at the office, coming home to eat alone. He avoided contact with Geoff or discussion about him.

The day after Dirk's stormy visit Geoff came home early from the university. He tried to explain once again to Marcia how sorry he was for the hurt he'd caused her, but why he could not take his father's position.

Marcia refused to listen; her guilt over her disloyalty to Piet was still too raw for her to be objective. "Let's forget the whole thing ever happened Geoff," she remonstrated. "Your main responsibility now is to finish school. You've caused your father a lot of embarrassment at work and even jeopardized his position with Dirk. Let's hope you've learned your lesson through all this."

Seeing her attitude, Geoff drew back into his own shell, and for the next few days she saw little of him. He left for school early in the morning and would excuse himself from the dinner table, mumbling something about working on a paper due before Monday.

Ouma's constant criticism and daily review of the whole demonstration incident wore on Marcia's nerves like rubbing a bruise. In Ouma's mind, Moses' laziness was all the proof she needed to confirm her conviction that Dirk Retief was absolutely right and any retreat from the nationalist policies was not only foolish but immoral. "Geoff should be ashamed of himself, disgracing the family and his Afrikaans tradition like that," she said imperiously.

Only Tim and Gary's boisterous chatter about sports, their insatiable teasing, and their innocent concentration on things like food, rugby, and girls, gave Marcia a sense of normalcy.

Almost a week had passed since Ouma had fired Moses, and the garden was showing signs of neglect. Ouma prided herself in manicured lawns, meticulously trimmed hedges and bushes, and flower beds that looked like a picture from a gardening magazine. But this took daily attention.

"If only I had one of my boys from the farm here," Ouma lamented. "Oupa made them work. They weren't spoiled like these city natives who just want an easy job. Don't they have country boys coming into the Bantu Affairs office in town that need jobs?"

By Friday Marcia realized that there'd be no peace until she made some effort to find another gardener. She and Ouma had just finished their morning tea out on the patio and Ouma had gone off to pick some dahlias which were producing their last splurge of the season, when Marcia heard the doorbell ring. A few moments later Angeline came to call her, a surprised expression on her face.

"Ma'am, there's a black girl at the front door asking for you. I told her to come around to the back door, but she said she'd wait for you on the front step."

Cheeky, thought Marcia to herself. Respectable Africans did not appear at the front doors of white residences. But many of the younger, city-bred blacks had forgotten their place these days.

"What does she want, Angeline?"

"She didn't say, madam. She just said to tell you her name is Thandi."

Alarmed, Marcia jumped to her feet. Glancing

in the garden to see if Ouma was still preoccupied with her flowers, Marcia hurried to the front door.

What gall, she thought. *Doesn't she know we've had enough trouble about that stupid demonstration already? What can she want now?*

Thandi was standing quietly outside the screen door, contemplating her black oxfords and the layer of dust that now hid the luster of a vigorous shine. She was dressed in a neatly pressed pleated brown skirt, a white blouse, and a beige blazer. The black tam on her head gave her the appearance of a schoolgirl, but the troubled brown eyes had the look of a much older woman.

She made no effort to come in, nor did Marcia invite her. She could not bring herself to return the hospitality she had been offered in Soweto just a few days earlier.

"Yes?" Marcia asked, her voice sounding cold and officious. "What can I do for you?"

An almost imperceptible tear glistened in Thandi's eyes as she lifted her face to directly meet Marcia's cold glance, and her voice was barely audible. "I've come to ask for help." She hesitated and contemplated her shoes again. "We found my brother Jacob yesterday. He's been in jail because he was caught without a pass."

Marcia almost sighed audibly. At least it wasn't more trouble for Geoff!

"I'm glad to hear he's safe," Marcia volunteered.

"Some friends at the Family Commission paid his fine, but he's got to leave Johannesburg in seventy-two hours unless he can find a job. My mother is so upset. She's been too sick to work regularly, and she needs Jacob here to help the family. But," she added in desperation, "I've spoken to all my friends and no one has a job for him. If I don't find something this weekend, he'll have to go back to the country on Monday. And there's no work there. He's a good worker, Mrs. Steyn. He could learn to do anything."

Marcia's first reaction was to send the girl away. She wanted nothing more to do with the Ngubanes. The guilt over her trip out to Soweto added to her concern about Geoff and Piet. This would just complicate things more.

Through the open screen door she heard the murmur of women's voices coming from around the house. Ouma and her neighbor were having one of their over-the-fence chats. No doubt Ouma was pouring out her tale of woe about her gardener into the sympathetic ears of Mrs. Van Rooyen.

Then the thought struck her: maybe this was the answer to Ouma's gardener problem. If Thandi's brother was from the country, he wouldn't have the attitudes and bad working habits of the city, so that would be a mark in his favor in Ouma's eyes. And he wouldn't expect an inflated wage either.

"Just a minute, Thandi," she interjected. "It may be that my mother-in-law would give your brother a job in the garden. What did you say his name was?"

"Jacob, madam," Thandi responded, a note of hope in her voice.

Marcia returned a few minutes later with the news that Ouma had agreed to give Jacob a try to see if he would be suitable.

"Mrs. Steyn is very particular about her garden, so Jacob will have to learn well and work hard," she warned. "She's fired three gardeners this summer already. Jacob better be on time and come prepared to work."

"I'm sure he'll do his best. Thank you, madam."

"Tell Jacob to be here at eight o'clock Monday morning. I'll have to take him down to the Bantu Affairs Department to register him. Make sure that he brings his temporary permit with him."

"I'll tell him." Then as she turned to leave, she asked softly, "Is everything all right with Geoff?"

Anger welled up in Marcia as Thandi's question brought back the realities of the hurt and tension of the last few days. She also couldn't believe she had allowed herself to get involved again with Thandi, who Marcia felt was the cause of all the trouble in the first place.

Coldly she replied, "Master Goeff's indiscretions have caused us all a great deal of trouble. But he's come to his senses . . . and I certainly hope you have, too."

For a moment Thandi stared back at Marcia, intuitively aware that she must not say any more.

"Well, I'm glad he didn't get into any more trouble. I'll be sure Jacob is here early Monday morning." She turned and began her long walk back to the African bus stop where she would wait for the familiar green bus to take her back to Soweto.

As Marcia watched her move down the street, she was tempted to call her back, to tell her she'd changed her mind. But then she sighed and went back into the house, a strange uneasiness creeping over her — as though she'd opened a door she could never shut.

SIX
The Permit

Jacob arrived before eight o'clock on Monday morning. He stood uncomfortably on the back step, looking down at the gray shapeless hat in his hands, which he fingered and turned like a rosary.

Marcia watched him as Ouma grilled him about his work experience. She was almost embarrassed by her mother-in-law's harshness.

"Now, boy, if you work here, I'll have none of that laziness I've had before. When you're here, you work, do you understand?"

Jacob looked down at his battered hat, his voice barely perceptible as he murmured, "Yes, madam." He looked much younger than Marcia had expected, but then these blacks never looked their age. His body was girlishly slim, and his cheeks and chin were beardless. Even when he lifted his head so she could see his deep-set brown eyes fringed with thick long lashes, there was no sign of any emotion — no fear, no eagerness, no respect. It was as if he wore a film over his eyes, making them expressionless, exposing nothing and protecting the recesses of his heart.

He looks like a child, mused Marcia, *until you see his eyes. I wonder what we're letting ourselves in for!*

But to Ouma the boy's reaction seemed to spell conforming respect, and when she learned that he had worked some time for a white farmer's wife in the Free State where he'd lived with his granny, she was elated.

"That's good, boy, that's good."

Even when she offered him a pitifully low salary, less than she'd given Moses, Jacob showed no reaction. *No doubt he knows he hasn't any other choice,* thought Marcia. She determined to encourage Ouma to raise the amount after he'd proven himself.

The ride down to the Bantu Affairs Department in Johannesburg was silent. Jacob sat meekly in the backseat, responding in monosyllables whenever Marcia tried to start up a conversation.

"Did you bring your temporary permit?"

"Yes, madam."

"How long did it take you to get to our place?"

"Two hours, madam."

"Were the buses crowded?"

"Yes, madam."

Giving up the effort, Marcia concentrated on her driving in the rush hour traffic, which grew heavier as she neared the center of the city. Fortunately she was able to find a parking spot in the already crowded lot.

Jacob trailed behind her at a respectable distance as she wound her way across the lot and along the sidewalk toward the front door. Hundreds of blacks milled around on the sidewalks, but this was not the usual blustery high-spirited crowd she was used to seeing on the streets of Johannesburg.

She just took for granted that wherever blacks gathered, they would shout and laugh. She had marveled at how they seemed to know so many people, stopping to talk to friends and acquaintances wherever they were. It struck Marcia that she could go shopping time after time in the city and not meet one person she knew. And yet these people always seemed to find someone to talk to.

But here at the Bantu Affairs Department, the people seemed more subdued as they waited in a line that snaked out of the door and around the corner of the red brick building at the end of the block.

People seemed resigned to spending another frustrating day of endless red tape and bureaucracy. Ambitious vendors had already set out their wares hoping to attract customers from the captive crowds in the slow moving lines. A group of people was gathered around a cart selling greasy looking fat cakes and dusty bottles of cold drink. *There are always entrepreneurs who can take advantage of any situation,* thought Marcia amused.

Jacob trailed hesitantly behind her, perhaps not wanting to be seen with a white woman. Marcia felt conspicuous in this mass of black humanity. She lifted her chin and tried to ignore the sullen stares of the men lounging against the building and the questioning glances of those squatting at the curb throwing dice to pass the endless hours.

"Madam," a smiling, open-faced boy called, jumping to his feet from where he'd been lounging against the building. "You want a gardenboy? I have experience."

Marcia just shook her head, keeping her eyes straight ahead. No one had to tell her she didn't belong, that she was out of place. But although she felt uncomfortable she wasn't afraid. She was simply in an alien world.

The Office of Bantu Affairs established the perimeters of the lives of African people in Johannesburg. It determined who could and couldn't live and work there or have a house there. All hinged on the precious pass that was issued at the Bantu Affairs office — the most important document for any African; one that he or she must carry at all times. The pass proved legal residency in the city. An employer had to sign it monthly to legalize the worker's rights in the city; a job was required for any African to stay.

Marcia had often heard Pieter explain the value of the pass system: "Without it, we'd have every Bantu in the country coming to Johannesburg. Can you imagine the slums, the unemployment, the crime? By allowing only blacks with passes to stay in the city, we're protecting the standard of living for the blacks that are here legally. It's for their good — though heaven knows, they don't act like it."

Though Marcia had never been to the Office of

Bantu Affairs before, she knew that she would not have to stand in the line that wound around the corner and seemed as immovable as a traffic jam. Some of her friends who'd helped their servants with passes had told her, "If you go with your worker, they'll take care of you right away. But if you send him or her to get it sorted out, your worker will lose three days' work standing in lines."

Marcia felt uncomfortable as she entered the pass offices. The resentment was thick enough to cut as she pushed past those crowding the doorway, muttering a polite "Excuse me." For a moment she hesitated to enter the room that was filled with the acrid smells of unwashed bodies and clothes.

There was a depressed atmosphere hovering over those waiting in the office; a veneer of compliant respect camouflaged the feelings of those who knew no other way to protest the bureaucracy they had come to accept with resignation. People spoke quietly to each other or stood in stony silence as they listened to the clerks issue commands in clipped Africaans.

It must be hard on the children, thought Marcia, as she saw a little one tugging on his mother's skirts. A baby wailed helplessly while its mother, busy talking, jogged her on her back. Finally she untied the blanket that held the baby on her back and slipped her around to the front. Nonchalantly she unbuttoned her blouse and offered the child her breast heavy with milk.

An old patriarch leaned on his nobkirri (a cane

with heavy knob at the top), a weary look on his wrinkled face under a crown of white hair. His tattered black jacket hung to his knees, the collar frayed so that the rough edges of the inner lining rubbed his neck. He wore no shoes on his calloused feet. Marcia wondered how long he'd been standing in the line. Then she saw a youngster, wearing an equally tattered shirt and patched khaki shorts, bring the old man a mug of water. There was a glow of love as the rheumy eyes lit up with gratitude. The boy helped the old man move over to the wall where he settled on the floor, and the boy returned to take his place in line.

Marcia was surprised to see the number of well-dressed blacks mixed in the crowd. One distinguished-looking man stood ramrod straight, his expensive leather briefcase caught between his spotlessly polished shoes. He seemed impervious to the confusion around him.

Marcia had thought only country people looking for permits to do laboring jobs stood in these lines. But it seemed here at the commission everyone was reduced to the lowest common denominator — everyone who was black, that is.

A harsh voice rang out over the rumble of voices: "Keep the line moving, or I'll close the window for today."

Marcia saw the order had come from behind the heavy grilled partition above the chest-high counter that separated the people who were in the lines from the clerks behind the counter.

She could see two young white men talking to each other, while the elderly man who had

shouted the command stood at the desk filling in
a long sheaf of papers before him. Everywhere
there were files piled, waiting to be returned to the
rows of shelves behind the counter. *How do they
ever find anything!* Marcia wondered. A black girl
in a blue striped uniform passed a tray with steaming cups of tea to the clerks, and the two younger
men stopped to drink, moving away from their
desks.

One of the clerks had been dealing with a
woman who had obviously just come from the
country. Her hair was piled high in a Zulu "bee-
hive" made stiff with red ocher mud and decorated
with beads. She wore more heavy beadwork on her
arms and around her neck, and bright colored
cloths were draped circumspectly over her shoulders covering her breasts. The man standing beside her was obviously her husband. *He's probably
trying to get a permit for her to come and live in
the city with him*, thought Marcia. But from the
distressed looks on their faces he had been unsuc-
cessful.

Just then a tall black policeman, dressed in an
immaculate khaki uniform with glistening brass
buttons and insignia, approached her. "Madam
can go up to the counter on the other side. Someone will help you right away." He pointed to a door
leading to another room.

Embarrassed, Marcia moved forward through
the crowd. She felt as though she was walking on
stage before a hostile audience. She would have
given anything to have dropped out of sight at that
moment.

But instead, she turned to Jacob, who looked as though he felt the same way and urged him forward. "Come along, Jacob, we may as well get this over with."

Later that evening Marcia told her family of the experience. She could still feel the hostile gaze of the hundreds of eyes turned upon her as she had explained Jacob's situation and requested a work permit.

"But they gave it to me without any problem at all," she concluded. "They were actually very nice to me. And Jacob seemed really grateful for the job. He certainly worked hard the rest of the afternoon, didn't he, Ouma?"

Piet didn't seem to want to dwell on the subject of the gardenboy this evening. He quickly changed the subject and began telling Marcia about his day's events, something he hadn't had time to do lately.

Later in the living room over coffee he shared exciting news. "Dirk's campaign is going very well. Several members of the parliament have endorsed his candidacy, and even the prime minister has sent him a letter of encouragement. He wants me to appear with him at a civic function next week. In fact, Anna will be going along so people can meet her. I think it would be nice for you to be there, too."

"Do you think Dirk would want me?" she asked, conscious that her English background was sometimes an embarrassment to Piet's Afrikaans friends.

"Oh, he especially asked that you come along.

You're very attractive, Marci. He'll be proud to have you in his campaign." He pulled her toward him with a gentle hug and added, "And so will I."

Marcia hadn't heard Pieter use that endearing pet name in ages. It brought her a warm glow of happiness and contentment. For a moment she rested her head on his shoulder, smelling the faint aroma of after-shave that was uniquely his.

What a comfortable, relaxed place to be, she thought, hoping there would be no more disrupting scenes with Geoff. Marcia knew this campaign of Dirk's could open up a whole new world for their own family. *Dirk appreciates and needs Piet,* she thought with satisfaction. *He might even ask him to come to Capetown to help him once he's elected.*

She smiled at her husband. "Oh, Piet, I'm so glad for you. I'll try to help as best I can. Is there anything else I can do besides buy a new dress for the campaign?"

"Just be sure the dress is blue."

They could laugh now about the blue dress. It had become a standing joke between them. But it had marked their first serious quarrel in the early months of their marriage. It had all started out with a sale, a fantastic closing out sale that Marcia couldn't resist even though they were living on a very tight budget. . . . When Piet had offered, shortly after they were married, to work out their finances, Marcia had readily agreed. "You balance the checkbook, and I'll spend the money."

"Oh no you don't," Piet had retorted in a mocking yet firm tone. "If you're going to quit teaching at the end of the year so we can start our family, we'll have to save every cent we can get."

Marcia's expenses had been minimal while she lived at home with her parents, so her small teaching salary had been enough for the fun things she'd wanted to do. And, of course, Daddy had always been ready to bail her out when a check bounced.

But after her marriage her income became part of a budget, and she was restricted to "pocket money." And the little blue dress that she saw and loved didn't quite fit that category, even at its rock bottom price.

She had gone into the shop to try it on "just for fun." Then as she admired herself in the mirror, Marcia had felt a niggling resentment. *Why shouldn't I be able to buy a dress when I want it? After all, I do earn the money.*

Impulsively she had turned to the hovering sales clerk and said, "I'll take it."

She'd decided she'd surprise Piet and wear the new dress that Friday evening at dinner at Piet's brother Jacobus' house. Andrea, his wife, worked in an insurance agency and had exquisite taste in clothes; Marcia always felt a bit dowdy around her.

She had just been putting on the finishing touches to her makeup, admiring how the blue of the dress gave her gray eyes a deeper hue, when Piet came into the bedroom.

There had been an awkward pause, then Marcia twirled around. "How do I look?" But the admiring smile she'd expected didn't develop.

"Where did you get that dress?" There had been

an unmistakable anger in Piet's soft-spoken question.

"I bought it. It was a fantastic bargain."

"What did you buy it with?"

Piet's judgmental tone had sparked Marcia's anger.

"With my money—what else?"

"Your money? I thought we agreed it was all ours now."

"Well, I should have some right to spend it then."

"According to our budget, you spend plenty of it."

"But only what you tell me to spend."

Marcia remembered how the angry tears had welled up in her eyes as she pulled the offending dress over her head.

"I guess you have to have your own way in this, too. I'll take it back and tell the clerk my husband won't let me keep the dress."

She'd thrown it disdainfully on the bed and rummaged angrily through her closet. The bedroom door had slammed behind her as Piet called back, "We have to leave in five minutes."

On the way to Jacobus's house they had sat in stony silence, looking straight ahead, neither ready to make the first move.

Then Marcia had begun feeling ridiculous; her anger had worn off and she realized she'd over-reacted. After all, she had agreed to their budget. She wanted the baby as much or more than Piet did.

She'd looked ruefully down at herself and then glanced over at Piet just in time to catch his eye. Suddenly they both had burst into uncontrollable laughter. Bubbling with mirth, Marcia had managed to ask, "Piet, can we turn around and go home so I can change?"

Piet had pulled over to the side of the road and shut off the car. "We'll be late, but first let me look at you. Wherever did you find that getup?"

Marcia recalled looking down at herself and realizing just how ridiculous she looked. She had pulled an old high school uniform she'd kept for sentimental reasons out of the back of the closet. It was too short and too tight. It even had a patch on the shoulder where she'd torn it taking a short-cut through the neighbor's backyard.

She had reached over to take Piet's face between her hands. "I've been foolish. . . . I'd be more embarrassed than you to arrive at Andrea's dressed like this." They made up and returned home so she could change. But she ended up keeping the blue dress — somehow they had found some elastic in their budget.

These days budgets weren't a problem, and Piet was often the one to encourage her to get a new outfit. "Actually, it doesn't have to be blue," he teased, "just so it's not uniform gray."

Then he grew more serious. "But besides buying a new dress, I think we should invite Dirk and Anna for dinner. I think after the last time he was here, he needs to know he's welcome as a friend."

They spent the next hour talking about Dirk's campaign and how they would fit into it. Pieter even agreed that they should invite Dominee Van Rensburg and his wife to the dinner, too, since Dirk was working on getting his influential backing.

"I'll make sure the boys all have other plans, so there won't be any distractions," Marcia assured Pieter. *Or any more scenes with Geoff*, she added to herself.

The tensions of the past few weeks seemed to have slipped away, and Marcia resolved that she would do all she could to keep anything from destroying their peace again. Little did she realize that they were in a lull before an even greater storm to come.

SEVEN
The Letter

The morning sun poured into the bedroom, and Marcia was conscious of its warmth even before she opened her eyes. *Pieter must have left for the office without waking me,* she thought dreamily, savoring the cozy comfort of those lazy moments before she had to pull herself into the day.

The bedroom door opened quietly, and Pieter whispered tentatively, "Honey, are you awake?"

"Mmm." Marcia nodded drowsily. "Just barely."

Pieter came over to the bed and bent down to kiss her. He smelled of soap and after-shave, and she reached her arms around his neck to pull him down toward her.

"Hey," he laughed, "I'd love to stay, but I'm late now. Just came in to see if you were awake. Can you be sure to get the electric bill paid today? It was due yesterday, and I haven't had a chance to write a check."

Marcia playfully nuzzled his neck as Pieter pulled away from her. "I've really got to run. See you tonight."

Ever since their long talk the other night, Marcia could sense a change in Pieter. It was almost like the early days of their marriage. He was more relaxed and yet so excited about all the possibilities of the campaign. "I wonder if he's seeing himself as a candidate in a few years?" Marcia asked herself. "Dirk is certainly setting him up for something. The dinner tomorrow night may be more important than just mending fences."

She suddenly realized all she had to do and jumped out of bed. She sat down at her desk and began making lists.

Through her bedroom window the garden looked beautiful in the morning sunshine. She could see Jacob digging around the roses that still bloom profusely late in the season. Jacob was a quiet sort; he'd been here a week already, and she'd hardly spoken two words with him. Ouma gave him his instructions every morning, and she hadn't complained too much about how he carried them out. Oh, there was the usual, of course — that he was slow, that she had to tell him the same thing three times over before he caught on. But if Ouma didn't complain more than that, he must be a fairly good worker.

As Jacob straightened up, he glanced back at the house. Marcia suddenly remembered that he hadn't had any breakfast yet. Angeline usually saw to it that he had something to eat shortly after he came to work, but this was her day off. Marcia realized he must be starved and thirsty working out there in the hot sun.

Angeline usually cooked a big pot of porridge for herself and for Jacob, but Marcia wasn't about to do that. Quickly dressing, she hurried down the hall to the kitchen. *I'd better fix something for Jacob before I do anything else*, she thought. She pulled an aluminum plate and mug out from under the sink where Angeline kept the servants' dishes, and filled the mug with hot steaming tea, adding three heaping spoons of sugar. She cut two thick slabs of white bread, smeared them with jam, and then on impulse grabbed an orange out of the bowl on the cupboard. *That'll make up for the porridge*, she thought.

"Jacob!" Her voice rang out through the clear morning air. "Your breakfast's ready."

She watched him finish digging around the roses where he was working, then drop his shovel and amble back to the house. He wasn't a bad looking lad, though not as good-looking as his sister Thandi. His nose was broad, set in a rather round face with full cheeks and thick Negroid lips. But his eyes were soft and expressive. He wore his thick curly hair in a modified Afro, cut almost flat across the top of his head. From his appearance she could not have guessed his age, but from his documents she knew he was twenty years old.

He stood outside the kitchen door, rubbing his hand on his patched brown overalls, waiting for her to bring his food. She couldn't tell if the look on his face was sullen because he was hungry or simply reserved because she was white.

"I'm sorry you had to wait so long, Jacob. I forgot that Angeline wasn't here today. I've just fixed bread and jam, and here's an orange. Is that all right?"

Jacob's coarse mud-stained hands reached out and he took the plate and mug from her. "Yes, madam," was all he allowed to escape.

He turned to go toward the big shade tree under which he usually sat to eat his food, but Marcia called to him once again.

"Jacob, I've hardly had a chance to talk to you since we got your pass fixed up the other day. Madam Steyn says you're doing well. Are you happy here?"

"Yes, madam."

Marcia stepped outside the kitchen door, an unexplained determination taking hold of her to make contact with this uncommunicative boy.

"How is Thandi? Is she back at work?" There was almost an imploring tone to her voice.

"Yes, madam. She is back."

"Is your mother looking for work again?"

A light turned on in Jacob's eyes as he looked into her face for the first time. "My mother is not working madam. Now that I am back home and have a job, she is able to stay home."

Marcia detected a note of pride in his voice. "Isn't she fortunate to have such a reliable son to take over the family responsibilities!" She could have kicked herself for her condescending tone of voice. Why couldn't she talk to him as an ordinary person? She tried again.

"I heard your mother isn't well. Thandi told me

she'd quit her job. How is she feeling now?"

"She's feeling better, madam." But then another signal leapt from his warm brown eyes, and a troubled look spread over his face as he added, "She never complains, but I hear her moaning in her sleep. She needs to go to the hospital to see the doctor, but she won't go."

He stopped, as if he'd exposed too much of his real self to this white woman who had everything and couldn't possibly care how his mother felt. Jacob turned and walked toward the big tree to eat his breakfast.

Startled, Marcia realized he was worried about his mother, just like Geoff would worry about her if she were sick. She wanted to ask more questions, but it was clear he had closed the conversation. So she simply called after him, "I hope she'll be all right," and walked back into the house.

Marcia soon forgot about Jacob and his family as she spent the next hour making lists for Angeline—clean the silver, iron the linen cloth, make milk tarts—and planning an elaborate menu. When she finished, her shopping list looked formidable.

Having geared up for the day's tasks, Marcia hurried down the hall to pick up her bag, her lists clutched purposefully in her hand. She remembered other shopping expeditions when her lists were left lying forgotten on the kitchen table while she bought what she didn't need and forgot what she did.

Ready to go, she called to Ouma, who was sitting on the patio enjoying the warmth of the morning sun. "I'm off to go shopping, Ouma. I'll be back by lunchtime."

Halfway out the door, she stopped herself. "Oops, I almost left Geoff's blazer again. He asked me to take it to the dry cleaner last week."

She hadn't been in Geoff's room for a while. Angeline cleaned it every day, and he kept his door shut—just like he'd shut himself away from her the last few weeks. She didn't want to take sides in the conflict between him and Piet. But she was torn—her visit to Soweto had shaken up a lot of her preconceptions. And the more she studied the Bible, the more clear the requirement for treating others with love and justice became.

She wished they could discuss these prickly questions unemotionally, but that seemed to be impossible. So she decided to try to stay neutral on the issue that divided the men she loved.

Yet, as she and Pieter shared more and more in the exciting new political opportunities before him, it seemed Geoff pulled farther and farther out of their family circle. Marcia shook her head sadly as she went into Geoff's room. He had left it clean and organized, in contrast to Tim and Gary's room which always looked like a whirlwind had blown through it. Geoff's bed was made up, even though Angeline hadn't been here today to do it. His textbooks were lined precisely on the shelf above his desk, his papers stacked neatly. One book lay open on the desk, a pencil lying across the page where he'd been marking passages.

Marcia sighed with concern. Geoff was such a hard-working student. It would be a shame if he al-

lowed political entanglements to interfere with
his education.

She was relieved to find the blazer with the Wits
emblem hanging right in the front of the closet.
He wore it almost every day to school, even
though it needed cleaning. *It's a good thing we had
those leather patches put on the elbows, or it
would be worn through by now*, she thought as she
rummaged through the pockets to remove Geoff's
things before she took it.

Marcia pulled a pen and handkerchief from one
pocket, some loose change from another. She felt
carefully in the inside pockets, not wanting to
miss things tucked away in the deep inner lining
as she had done in the past, causing the boys to
complain when some paper or object was ruined.
She'd learned not to take these bits and pieces of
paper, which sometimes represented treasures,
lightly.

Reaching down into the deepest of the inside
pockets, she pulled out a folded piece of paper
she'd almost missed. She was about to put it on the
desk with the other accumulated debris when the
signature caught her eye.

Marcia had made it a rule never to read her children's private correspondence, and she'd taught
them to respect each other's privacy, too. So for a
moment she pulled her eyes away from the in-
criminating words, but a sense of fear and outrage
overwhelmed her. She picked the handwritten
note up again to be sure she'd read the name cor-
rectly, then slowly unfolded the note — just a half
sheet of paper torn from a notebook — and read it.

"Dear Geoff, don't come to see me at the office today. We have taken on a new part-time worker. I won't be alone this afternoon. Besides, I'm afraid you'll get into more trouble if anyone should find out we've been meeting. You've had enough problems without me. I'm sending this note with Jacob. He says you usually come by to greet him when you leave for school. Thandi."

"Oh, God," Marcia said and sank down on the bed, horrified. She stared at the note in her hand with unbelieving eyes. What did this mean? How long had Geoff and Thandi been meeting? Maybe the police were already watching them. The Immorality Act was designed to prevent interracial marriages, and it was even illegal for a white and black to sleep together.

Marcia groaned aloud. Surely it hadn't come to that! Marcia had had a feeling about Thandi the first time she saw her in Soweto. She'd probably set her cap for Geoff right from the start. But why? They couldn't date; they couldn't marry; they couldn't even live together. It was wrong, all wrong. Marcia lay back on the bed, desperate tears streaming down her face.

She didn't know how long she lay shaking on the bed, but the shrill ring of the telephone down the hall brought her to her senses. She was grateful when the ringing stopped; she couldn't have answered it now for anything. She just continued to slump on the bed, mutely staring at the crumpled note that had shattered the sense of euphoria that had enveloped her the past few days.

For a moment she was tempted to crush the

note in her hands and throw it on Geoff's bed, to let him worry about who had found it or what the consequences would be. Then her good sense took over. Carefully she smoothed the note and folded it as she'd found it. She slipped it in among the other papers that she'd taken from Geoff's pockets, as if she'd pulled them all out together and left them for him as she usually did.

She needed time to think and get herself under control. To mishandle this situation could mean the end not only of Piet's career, but of their whole family. She picked up her bag and the blazer from where it had fallen on the floor and wearily shut the bedroom door behind her. She still had a lot to do for the gala dinner for Dirk and Anna and the Dominee and his wife. But the anticipation had turned sour.

EIGHT
The Dinner

The dinner went well. Marcia could tell from
Piet's relaxed manner and tone of voice as he led
the way into the lounge for coffee that he was enjoying himself. It was too early in the season for a
fire in the fireplace, but the roses Ouma had ar-
ranged on the mantle added a golden touch to the
soft beiges and browns of the room. The chairs
were grouped invitingly around the coffee table
which was laid out with Marcia's best china on
one of Ouma's exquisite hand-crocheted doilies.

Her guests settled down comfortably while
Marcia poured coffee. The Dominee's hearty
laugh forced a smile to her lips in spite of herself.
There was a buoyancy and vitality in Dominee
Van Rensberg that drew people to him, and it
seemed only natural for him to take the lead in the
conversation.

The Dominee was a tall, well-built man with a

shock of thick prematurely gray hair and blue eyes that penetrated as though he could read people's thoughts. He had a gift of making everyone feel comfortable in his presence, unless of course he was bringing them to task for their mortal sins. But tonight in the company of a future parliament member and a prominent (if uninvolved) family in his congregation, he exuded charm and carried the conversation along with his rich storehouse of stories.

Tina his wife had the same air of self-confidence. Her blonde hair was sculptured by a master hairdresser, her nails beautifully mani-cured, her complexion — like that of so many Afrikaans women — was flawless and radiated good health. Marcia could imagine that her phone rang constantly as worried or distressed women in the church called her for advice. She had never been in Tina's home, but she was sure it ran like clockwork, with servants trained to keep the household moving on well-oiled wheels of dis-cipline.

But though Tina was capable and independent, she "knew her place" and quietly sipped her cof-fee, letting her husband carry the bulk of the con-versation. In fact, except for exchanges about their children, the women had contributed little to the evening's conversation; it had been dominated by the overriding political concerns of Dirk's campaign.

The way so many South African men pampered and protected their wives — keeping many of them like perennially spoiled children — had always irritated Marcia. She was thankful that Piet respected her opinions and encouraged her to get involved in new things. In fact, lately he'd been urging her to go back to teaching. "The boys are away all day," he'd said. "It's a shame to waste your qualifications and experience."

But somehow the men's condescension didn't bother Marcia tonight as it usually did. Over the last few days she had steeled herself not to think beyond the mechanics of the dinner. She wanted it to go well for Pieter and was relieved she didn't have to make any further effort. Rather the three men were infused with a sense of success and challenge as they considered the possibilities of the next election. The Dominee was as keen as the others to promote Dirk's cause in his parish.

As they moved from the dining room to the lounge for coffee, the Dominee hardly missed a beat in the story he'd begun around the table.

"Ya, my grandmother was one of the 26,000 women and children who died in the British concentration camps during the Boer War."

"How terrible," murmured Dirk's wife. "Do you know how she died?"

"I think she simply starved to death. Many times my father told us children of how she kept them alive by giving up her own food rations. He sat by her cot in the tent in the blazing summer heat and watched her breathe her last. He never had any love for the British I can tell you."

A faraway look came into the Dominee's eyes and he nodded his head, "Ya. After that defeat our people determined never to be defeated again. My father often told me how he heard President Paul Kruger say that though the British had thousands in the field to the hundreds of Boers, the Afrikaaner nation had a supreme commander of heaven and earth, Jesus Christ. He believed that God was just testing the Afrikaaners to strengthen them."

There was silence for a moment as each pondered the valiant band of Dutch forefathers who had hung on so tenaciously to their destiny.

Then Pieter remarked quietly, "And now we may be fighting for our lives again. But this time it will be the blacks who want to take from us what we fought so hard to win. And there's no other place to go back to. The world can't seem to understand that this is our home. We have no other."

"Ah, our own young people don't understand," complained Dirk, rising agitatedly from his chair to pace up and down. "They seem to forget that when the Dutch first landed in the Cape in 1652, there weren't any black tribes there. The Afrikaaners worked hard to develop this nation by keeping its languages and traditions pure. The native tribes they met were primitive in every way. They could see from the beginning that the blacks were like children who could never run the country."

"Well, of course, Dirk," the Dominee interjected, "the apartheid laws were designed for the good of the blacks, too. No race would be pure today if we'd allowed inter-marriage and social mixing. But Chief Gatsha Buthelezi can't get it through his head that the only reason he can hold forth with his tribal leaders down there in Zulu-land, keeping the traditions of his Zulu heritage, is because apartheid laws protected the Zulu nation from destruction."

Dirk sank back into his chair again, shaking his head in perplexity. "Yet people like Van den Berg continue to criticize the Bantustan policy which was designed for that very reason," he said in a frustrated tone. "When all nine homelands have been granted independence, each tribe will have its own independent area where it can protect its heritage, and where people will have full rights to make their own laws."

At the mention of Van den Berg's name, Pieter looked apprehensively at Dirk, wondering if the subject of the ill-fated demonstration would come up. Marcia saw his look and was glad that Dirk was so intent on the Dominee's analysis that he didn't pick up on the sensitive subject. She was also relieved that Goeff wasn't here. She'd heard him hold forth against the Bantustan policy with scorn. "Why they've set aside 18 percent of the land as 'homelands' for more than 80 percent of the population — and it's the least productive and least accessible land in the country. Every black is to have his citizenship there, regardless of the fact that he may never have been there in his life. Do you call that fair?"

Usually Marcia ignored Geoff's tirades as just so much youthful exuberance. But since her visit to Soweto, Dirk and the Dominee's arguments seemed to have a hollow ring to them. She wished she dared ask how they would feel if their rights as citizens were taken away.

But, having warmed to his subject, Dominee Van Rensberg was unaware of the undercurrents in the room. "I believe we have a God-given responsibility to care for our natives," he stated, shaking his pipe in the air for emphasis. "And we do care for them. They have the highest standard of living in all of Africa. We're spending millions of rands on education, housing, and free hospitalization. You know, when Prime Minister Vervoerd made the statement in 1966 that he'd never seen a country where integration has worked, he was right."

Dirk laughed. "The USA would like to have you think it works, but they're always just a breath away from a race riot in one part of the country or another."

"I've heard about their so-called 'integrated' schools, where kids carry knives. One of my friends visited his brother in California. They have several teenage children. He says the kids wait to go to the toilet till they get home in the afternoon; they're afraid to go into the school restrooms because of the violence."

"We'd never allow that, never," the Dominee responded emphatically. "The Bible tells us to live at peace with all men. We Reformed theologians have long since come to the conclusion that it is impossible to live at peace in a racially mixed society."

"Furthermore, this nation was given us as our

due by God himself. Our founding fathers saw themselves as modern Hebrews, chosen of God, facing the enemy and gaining victory at God's hands. The life of this nation is in our hands. To integrate would be racial suicide, and that goes against all that Scripture teaches."

A flutter of clapping hands and an affirming "hear, hear" brought the Dominee back to the present. Embarrassed, he wiped his forehead with his folded handkerchief and placed it back in his pants pocket. "So sorry, for a minute I thought I was back in the pulpit."

The group laughed, and Pieter tried to cover the Dominee's embarrassment. "That's all right. If all your audiences were as fully in agreement with your sermons as we are, you'd have the biggest church in the country."

"Well, he wouldn't go over so well if he were speaking to a bunch of Wits students," remarked Dirk. "You heard they demonstrated the other day about housing in Soweto. Now I hear they want pass laws changed so that the natives can bring their wives and children from the country to live with them here in the city."

The Dominee sat forward in his chair, pointing the stem of his pipe at Dirk to reinforce his point, "I tell you, Wits is full of communist influence these days. The English-speaking press is playing right into their hands, too."

Tina put her cup down on the coffee table, "It does seem a shame that men have to be separated from their wives for such long times. But then I understand that they do this all over Africa. Evidently African women are used to being left home with the children."

"Or they leave the children with Granny and go off to work in the cities themselves," remarked Anna Retief. "My servant girl tried to keep her baby with her in her quarters, but we had to tell her she either had to send the child to her granny or the girl would have to find work elsewhere. She was constantly running back to the *ikhaya* to check on the child, or else we had a crying baby in the kitchen just when we had visitors."

"Where's her husband? Or does she even have one?" Tina asked.

"He works in Johannesburg and comes to see her once a month. He'd move in if we'd let him, but of course that's illegal. Even at that, I'm always worried there'll be a raid and we'll get into trouble for letting him stay overnight."

"I told you, Anna," Dirk spoke up, "he's allowed to stay seventy-two hours without a permit, as long as he is legally in the city."

He explained to the others, "We've had several raids in our neighborhood recently. There are just so many illegal Africans trying to get into the city. We simply don't have the jobs or housing to cope with them. The pass laws may seem harsh at times, but any law to be good has to have some teeth in it — and somebody gets bitten," he added almost defensively.

"But the alternatives are worse," conceded Dominee Van Rensberg. "We've had to make some very unpopular choices, which has turned the whole world against us. But one day I think everyone, black and white, will concede we had no other choices to make.

"We have to hold our own down here; the only country courageous enough to help us is Israel. The rest of the West is so hypocritical; they want our minerals — "

"And they're glad to let us hold the commies at bay in Angola and Southwest," interjected Dirk.

"But just let a few blacks get killed in a raid over the border when our border patrols chase the commies back, and we get front page headlines," Piet volunteered self-righteously.

As the men became more engrossed in their political analysis, Marcia's mind drifted. She had heard it all so many times before. But this time that uncomfortable niggling feeling persisted that everything wasn't ringing quite true, that perhaps there was another side to the story. Was there something they'd missed? Could they be fooling themselves?

What if she told them about the Ngubanes and her visit to Soweto? They'd think her unbalanced, like Geoff. She settled back with a sigh. She couldn't risk upsetting the happy accord tonight. *Just let this evening pass without incident*, she thought, as she smiled absently at Anna, who seemed totally absorbed in following the conversation. *I've got a far more serious problem to sort out . . . and I can't talk it over with anyone.*

N I N E
The Refusal

After the dinner, life settled down in the Steyn household. Geoff was busy preparing for exams. He seemed to use the house simply as a place to sleep, leaving early in the morning and working at the university library late every evening.

"I'm glad to see the boy put his mind to his work," responded Pieter when Marcia worried that he looked thin and was missing too many meals. "It won't hurt him to concentrate on his studies and forget all that black nonsense."

Though the contents of Thandi's note to Geoff was never far from Marcia's mind, there was no way she could confront him without revealing that she had read his private mail. Somehow she had the feeling that even if she told him that she knew about Thandi, it wouldn't make much difference. Geoff had left them; he lived in a different world. It was as though he and Pieter each spoke a different language that the other couldn't understand.

And Marcia was in the middle, carrying the weight of a secret she had to keep from both of them — a secret that clutched at her heart like a tightening vice.

She hardly admitted to herself that she made excuses for being in the yard or near the kitchen door in the mornings when Jacob arrived, watching through the window to see if Geoff stopped him or passed a note into his hands. She almost hated Jacob for his part in the whole sordid affair. Yet he was a good worker, faithful and diligent. He was quiet and kept to himself. She knew little more about him after a month than she had the day she took him to the Bantu Affairs Department for his pass.

Thus she was surprised to find him in conversation with Ouma outside the back door one bright morning when she came into the kitchen. He'd come even earlier than usual, so she hadn't been there when he'd arrived.

She couldn't make out Jacob's words, but Ouma's response was strident and clear. "No, my boy, we're not starting that. You get paid at the end of the month as I told you. I've always made it a policy not to forward advances to my servants. It just starts a bad habit. You've got to learn to manage your money like we Europeans do."

Unlike his usual quiet acquiescence, Marcia could hear the murmur of Jacob's response. She wanted to step nearer so she could understand what he was saying, but he and Ouma were standing right at the foot of the steps outside the open door and would see her eavesdropping.

Her voice tinged with impatience, Ouma broke in again. "Now don't get cheeky with me, boy. I just paid you last week, and I'm not going to advance another cent until the end of the month. There's no point in talking any more about it," and she turned up the stairs and into the kitchen, closing the door behind her.

Seeing Marcia, she shook her head. "They're all alike. They simply can't handle money. Can you imagine them running this country?"

"What did he want, Ouma?"

"He wanted a week's salary advanced. I told him I just paid him last week and I don't believe in advancing money. Before you know it, they don't have anything coming at the end of the month because they took it all out before they earned it. He'll just have to learn to think ahead."

"But what did he want it for?"

"He says he doesn't have enough to pay the rent; something about his mother being out of work. But it will be the same story all over again next month when the rent is due. I told him he has to set his rent money aside when he gets his pay, not spend it on a lot of foolish things and then not have enough to meet his bills."

"Perhaps this is something special, Ouma. His mother was working, but I understand she's been ill and has had to quit her job."

"Oh, these natives all have lots of relatives. He'll find an uncle or brother or someone to help out. I've watched this for years. The families seem to have money to help out when there's an emergency."

"You don't think you should have given it to him this once and told him it can't happen again?"

"That's just the way you spoil them, Marcia. I've had lots of years of experience working with these blacks. If you give them an inch, they'll take a mile." Then seeing Marcia's troubled face, her voice softened. "Don't worry child, he'll work it out with his family, you'll see. And he'll learn how to handle his money more wisely next month."

All that day Marcia was unable to get Jacob's disturbed pleading out of her mind. She knew what he was earning wouldn't go far for any foolishness. He had bus fare to pay to and from Soweto every day, and blacks had to pay as much for food as she did. Of course, they didn't eat as well—lots of mealie meal and mealie rice, and they probably didn't have meat very often. Admittedly she'd seen Jacob with a bottle of cold drink once in awhile, but then he should be able to buy a little luxury occasionally, too.

She wondered what rent cost for that little four-room house she had visited in Soweto. It did have electricity, which probably made it more expensive. And the toilet out in back had running water, but she didn't think they had it inside. Surely it couldn't cost much.

She wished she could ask Jacob, even give him the money herself. But she didn't dare interfere. This was Ouma's domain, and Pieter had made it very clear from the start that Ouma was to handle the garden and the gardener the way she wanted to.

"She doesn't have much left now that Pa is gone and the farm is sold," Pieter had said. "At least she'll have one area where she is solely in charge. And it will give her something to do and keep her out of your hair, too, Marci," he'd explained.

He was right of course. But Marcia still wondered how much the rent was and what would happen if the Ngubanes didn't pay it. Occasionally she'd read stories in the *Star* about evicted families. It was the kind of thing the Black Sash women demonstrated against and that the African Family Commission dealt with.

Marcia pondered the problem off and on most of the morning. She finally decided she would talk with Pieter. Perhaps he could persuade Ouma to help Jacob this one time. After all, he'd just had one month's salary since he started his job, and he couldn't be blamed for not having enough to cover all the living expenses, especially with a sick mother.

Later that day, Marcia was in Tim and Gary's room sorting socks when Ouma called down the passage to her. "Marcia, I'm ready."

"Coming," Marcia glanced at her watch. She'd completely forgotten that she'd promised to run Ouma over to a friend's house for tea. She glanced down at her white slacks and red and white striped top to see if they were "decent." *Guess I'll do*, she thought as she pushed her hair back from her face.

Grabbing the car keys off the hall table, she called to Angeline to tell her she would be gone for a half hour. But there was no response.

"Where's Angeline, Ouma?" she asked as she

slid behind the wheel of the front seat where Ouma was already settled and waiting.

"I sent her to the corner store for shampoo. I noticed I've run out and I want to wash my hair tonight. She should be back in a few minutes."

"Sometimes it takes her quite a while to walk down there. I guess she meets friends on the way. Anyway," Marcia started the engine, "I'll be back in half an hour and Jacob is in the yard, so I guess I needn't lock up."

As Marcia drove back after leaving Ouma at her friend's, she saw Angeline in deep conversation with another girl a block away from home. Marcia couldn't help smiling as she saw the two women burst out laughing about some shared story, their broad black faces wrinkling with mirth. *They're probably telling some story on "those foolish Europeans,"* she thought. *We probably seem as strange to them as they do to us.* She waved a greeting as she drove by. *I wonder if we are the main topic of conversation when they get together, like our servants seem to be when we're with our friends?*

Back at home, Marcia pushed open the front door, savoring the unusual solitude of the house, even for a few minutes. She loved its large relaxed rooms and the expansive view of the garden and pool through the French doors in the lounge. Somehow when the boys were all home every corner seemed lived in. But this afternoon it had that gracious welcoming look of a peaceful hideaway.

Suddenly Marcia stopped. Somewhere in the house she heard a door creak on its hinges. She

glanced at her watch; it was too early for Tim and
Gary to be home from school. Perhaps Geoff had
come home to study. No, his gray VW wasn't in the
driveway.

A twinge of fear gripped her heart. Just last week
a black had broken into a house less than a mile
away and surprised the owner in her bedroom. He
had pulled a knife and left the woman almost dead
before ransacking her bedroom and taking her
jewels.

Poised for flight, she forced herself to stop and
listen. Was she imagining something? No, there
was someone in her bedroom. The faint sound of a
drawer moving on its runners broke the silence.
She stifled the scream rising in her throat. She had
to get help without betraying her presence.

She would have to walk past her bedroom door
to get to the phone in the den. But then her escape
would be cut off if the intruder came out of her
room.

There was no one next door to help — her neighbors were working. Should she get Jacob? No, she
couldn't expect him to tackle a thief.

All these thoughts whirled through her mind as
she stood trembling in the passage, ready to run,
yet wanting to confront whomever dared to invade
her home.

Suddenly the bedroom door burst open.

Startled, Marcia screamed. A young black man
whirled around to face her, dropping a bundle of
clothes and her handbag.

"Jacob!" she cried out as she recognized him.
"You — you get out of this house right now!"

Hardly knowing what she was doing, Marcia threw the only thing she had in her hands — her car keys — at his head.

"Get out! And don't come back." Marcia chased the fleeing Jacob through the kitchen and out to the back steps.

"You ungrateful *kaffir.* You're just what Ouma's been telling me — you're all alike! I'm the one that's a fool for giving you and your sister a chance."

But Jacob was neither listening nor responding. He was gone. As her hysterical shouting dissolved into sobs, she collapsed on the back stoop, spent from the emotional encounter and shaking with fear and anger.

That night at supper her stunned family listened as Marcia recounted her frightening experience. "He didn't get away with anything. He dropped my purse in the hall. It had about twenty rand in it. I just can't believe he'd do such a thing!"

Pieter was grim-faced. "Did you call the police?"

"No, what good would it do? He didn't get anything."

Geoff, who for a rare occasion had joined them for supper, looked ashen as he listened to the discussion.

"It doesn't matter that he didn't take anything — he tried to," continued Pieter. "And he gave you a terrible fright. I'll report it anyway. They have a way of tracing these blokes down."

Then Pieter rose from the table as another thought struck him. "Did you check my gun? He may have taken that." He hurried down the hall to the bedroom.

"Did you hit him with the keys, Ma?" Tim teased. Tim and Gary savored the whole exciting drama.

"Naw, she couldn't throw that far," Greg retorted.

"Shut up, guys. This is nothing to joke about, Geoff interrupted. Turning to Marcia he asked, "You're not going to let Dad call the police, are you, Mom?"

Marcia stiffened and looked at Geoff coldly. "Why should I protect him? He broke his trust. Who knows where else he'll try this trick."

"You should have called right away, Marcia," Ouma said, shaking her head in anger.

In a few minutes Pieter returned relieved. "The gun's still there in the drawer next to the bed. Evidently he didn't get that far. After this Marcia, you really ought to learn how to use a gun. Dirk has insisted that Anna take lessons."

"Oh, I couldn't Piet. I was so scared this afternoon I would probably have shot myself if I'd had a gun."

"Can I learn, Dad, can I?" Greg burst in. "Some of the guys at school are going to classes on Saturday mornings."

Ignoring his youngest son's outburst of enthusiasm, Pieter continued, "That's just why you should take lessons. They'll teach you how to keep cool in a situation like that. In fact, they teach karate and other self-protection methods. It's not a bad idea at all in the climate we're living in these days."

The family sat around the dinner table longer than usual; the bizarre incident seemed to bring them all a little closer. All except Geoff, who excused himself saying, "I've got a quiz in the morning, so I'd better go to my room."

It was only after the boys and Ouma had settled in the den to watch TV and Pieter had left for a planning session for the campaign that Marcia had time to think through the afternoon's events by herself.

She could still see Jacob's startled face that instant when she'd recognized him and screamed his name. For one moment she thought she saw a look of beseeching, as if the cold mask he usually wore had fallen away and he wanted to open his heart to her. And then he'd dropped everything and run.

Could it be he was just so desperate? wondered Marcia. Maybe if Ouma had given him the advance this would never have happened. What should she have done? At the Bible study at Ruth's last week the question of helping the blacks came up in the discussion. Ruth had quoted a verse . . . what was it now? Something about "Masters give your servants what is just and equal." Some of the girls felt that certainly didn't mean the same salary as whites. But what was just? Shouldn't a man earn enough to be able to take care of his family?

Marcia shook her head as if to chase such treasonous thoughts from her mind. *It certainly isn't justice for Jacob to steal from us. He'll get what's coming to him for that.*

Suddenly Geoff broke into her reverie. "Mom, can I talk with you for a minute?" He dropped down on the floor next to her chair, like he used to as a little boy when they would have heart-to-heart talks.

"Sure Geoff. We don't have much time to talk these days, do we? You seem to be so busy at school. Are you ready for your quiz tomorrow?"

"Ya, as ready as I'll be I guess." There was a companionable silence for a moment, and then Geoff put his hand on her knee. "Mom, I think I know why Jacob went off his rocker today. Perhaps when you know what's happened at the Ngubanes', you won't be quite so hard on him."

Marcia stiffened. How dare he try to protect the Ngubane family? She was tempted to burst out that she knew all about him and his black girl-friend, but she couldn't. She just pinched her lips together and listened stoically as Geoff continued.

"This thing this afternoon was just out of desperation, Mom. Jacob is a really decent chap. You've noticed that yourself, haven't you?"

Marcia refused to be drawn in. She simply stared at her clenched hands in her lap.

"When Jacob came back to Jo'burg a few months ago, his mother had already been out of work for over a month. I don't know what's wrong with her, but Thandi says she has a lot of pain. The doctors haven't given her much to help her."

"Jacob told me about how his mother moans in the night," Marcia responded almost involuntarily, remembering the conversation in the garden with Jacob when his love for his mother broke down his usually impenetrable barrier.

"Well, I guess they really got into a lot of financial difficulty. Thandi only works part time, you know, since she's studying by correspondence through the University of South Africa. Her salary just couldn't keep up with all their expenses — rent, food, transportation."

"Then when Jacob was arrested for being without a pass, they had to scrape together enough bail to release him. The folks at the Family Commission helped, but they didn't do it all.

"Anyway, they're three months behind in their rent. The authorities issued a warrant last week that they had to make payment this week, or they would be put out."

Geoff grabbed her hands to make his point. "Mom, the police come and take the furniture out of the house and just put it on the sidewalk. They don't care that there's no place for the family to go. I guess Jacob just couldn't bear to see his mother put out on the streets, especially when she's so sick. You won't let Dad report him to the police, will you? I know I can't expect you to take him back. Maybe Thandi can find something else for him."

Marcia pulled her hands from Geoff's urgent clasp. "Why are you so interested in the Ngubane family, Geoff? There are lots of blacks who are in financial difficulty, but who don't resort to stealing. Why should Jacob get away with this just because they are having a little difficulty?"

Her voice sounded hard even to her own ears, and Geoff looked at her in disbelief. "But Mother, they're not just 'any blacks' —" He broke off, realizing he was saying more than he wanted to. He added lamely, "You've met Mrs. Ngubane, you know their situation. Doesn't that make any difference?"

Marcia pulled herself out of her chair and looked down at Geoff. "I'm not sure I understand everything that's going on here, Geoff. But I do know that what's wrong is wrong. I was going to try to convince Ouma to give Jacob an advance. If he hadn't broken his trust, he'd probably have had his rent payment tomorrow morning. But he chose to betray our trust and break the law. He'll have to pay the consequences."

Long after Geoff went back to his room and despite her determined words, Marcia sat staring into space, seeing Jacob's pleading face when Ouma refused his request and wondering which had been the greater wrong.

TEN
The Report

As soon as she saw the officers, she knew that Piet had reported the break-in.

They stood serious and unsmiling at the front door. The older one greeted her politely in Afrikaans, *"Goeie more, mevrou.* Your husband reported an attempted robbery by a Bantu?"

"Yes, yes, do come in." Marcia opened the screen door and stood back while the towering spokesman and his younger companion stepped into the front hall.

Though Marcia spoke Afrikaans fairly well, she reverted to English when she was under the least pressure; she couldn't add the burden of groping for words to the need to organize her thoughts.

"Please, come and sit down."

"No, thank you, madam, this will just take a moment," the leader responded in heavily accented English. He took out a notebook and pencil from inside his blue-gray jacket, around which he wore a broad leather belt and holster. The revolver he carried on his hip looked ready for business. A thick baton and handcuffs dangled from the other side.

If I didn't know better, I could be afraid of this no-nonsense man who is so organized for attack, Marcia thought.

"You say you caught this Bantu in your bedroom yesterday, madam? Why didn't you call right away?"

"I—I guess I was just too frightened, and relieved that he ran away without taking anything. But when I told my husband last night, he felt it should be reported to the police."

"Would you recognize this boy if you saw him again?"

"Oh yes. He . . . he was our gardener."

"Did he have his papers in order?"

"Yes, I took him to Bantu Affairs last month myself to get his pass."

The man looked knowingly at his younger partner. "Another one of these natives coming into the city looking for trouble."

As Marcia gave Jacob's name and address and repeated the details of the previous afternoon's break-in, she almost felt like a traitor. What would happen to Jacob now? Perhaps Geoff was right; perhaps he'd just acted out of desperation. But now he would certainly be arrested, and sent out of the city.

She heard herself asking, "What will you do if you find him?"

For the first time the younger man, who looked slim as a boy and whose smooth pink cheeks looked as though a razor had never touched them, broke in. "Don't worry madam, we'll find him. These *kaffirs* don't get away from us very easily."

"His punishment will be up to the judge, madam," interjected the older officer. "Certainly his pass to stay in Jo'burg will be revoked. Possibly he'll receive a sentence, though you say he didn't take anything. You'd better look around and make sure he hasn't gotten away with something without your noticing it. We'll get back to you when we locate him. It may take a little longer than usual because there are some problems out in Soweto and a lot of our security men are already on assignment."

"Are you expecting trouble?"

"No, no, it's nothing to worry about. We are maintaining a high profile out there. The students in the high school have been striking, and we heard rumors they were going to demonstrate." He closed his notebook as if to indicate he'd said enough.

As she closed the door behind the two officers, Marcia heaved a deep sigh. Why was she so confused? Jacob had broken into their home. It was Piet's duty to report the crime.

"A boy like that will just do the same thing to someone else, Marci," Piet had said last night as they got ready for bed. "And the next time the ending might not be so harmless."

So she'd agreed that he should call. But she hadn't said a word about Geoff's urgent appeal that they give Jacob another chance. She was still playing referee between the two of them, and she hated to bring up a suggestion that she knew would result in conflict.

Standing there in the front hall lost in her thoughts, she didn't realize the phone had rung until Angeline came out of the den. "Phone for you, madam."

She thanked Angeline and went to pick up the receiver. "Hello?"

"Marcia?"

"Oh, hello, Piet. I was just going to call you."

"Have the police come yet?"

"Yes, they just left."

"What are they going to do?"

"Oh, they said they'd find Jacob. They'll let us know when they do. But they said it might take a few days since there is something going on in Soweto. Have you heard anything about it?"

"Ya, some trouble in the high schools. The students are threatening to demonstrate, but I don't think it will come to anything. Listen, I called you about something else." Piet's voice sounded young and eager over the phone.

"Sounds like something good," she said, laughing, her mood changing with his.

"It is. Dirk and I have an appointment with the Minister of Education this afternoon in Pretoria. It's at three o'clock. Dirk has already left because he had some other people to see first. The press will probably be there since Dirk's campaign is getting a lot of attention in the news these days. It won't hurt our cause one bit to have such a powerful man as Van Heerden backing him."

"That's wonderful, Pieter."

"I'm wondering if you wouldn't like to come along for the ride, Marci. I can't invite you into the meeting of course, but you could window shop or something for an hour, and then we can go out to dinner over there. It would probably do you good to get out of the house."

"But what about the boys? I'd have to make arrangements for their supper."

"Ma can look after them. You know she's always looking for an excuse to be useful. I'll be home at one to pick you up, OK?"

"OK, Piet. I'll look forward to it."

Later, in the car, Marcia realized she had almost forgotten how beautiful the countryside was between Johannesburg and Pretoria. It was less than forty miles between the two cities, but Pretoria was bordering on the low veld and was more tropical than the mile high city of gold.

The farms still looked lush and green; the winter frosts hadn't turned the fields to brown yet. Sleek fat cattle grazed along the road, and here and there farmhouses — replicas of the beautiful Cape Dutch architecture — sat back from the road. Pieter had chosen a more scenic and a less traveled two-lane highway rather than the super highway. At one point they came to a crawl, blocked by a herd of cattle. The tattered herdsboy, flashing a happy-go-lucky smile, swatted the rumps of the lumbering beasts with a long stick to move them to one side of the road.

"Remember the time we cracked our windshield on the horns of one of those blokes when we were traveling through the Free State at night?" Pieter asked, breaking the companionable silence they'd been enjoying for the last mile or two.

"Do I remember! He just came out of nowhere. I never could figure out why farmers are allowed to move their herds along the public roads."

"It's much better than it used to be when all the cattle roamed free. I don't suppose we'll see this sight here in South Africa for too many more years, at least near the urban areas."

Since it was almost time for his appointment when they arrived in Pretoria, Pieter drove directly to the Union buildings.

"You can take the car and come back here to meet me in an hour and a half," he explained as he jumped out.

No matter how often Marcia came to Pretoria, the sight of the majestic sandstone Union building, sitting on the hilltop like a queen on her throne overlooking her subjects, took her breath away. The gardens, which spread out below a row of cannons built into the wall below the buildings, resembled a velvet green carpet with patterns of flower beds set like exquisite jewels into the lawn. Each season of the year boasted a different display as scores of gardeners cleared out the dying plants and transplanted another show of beauty.

Marcia could see a group of school children, dressed in their gray uniforms with white shirts and navy blazers, strolling along one of the paths two by two as their teacher explained the background of what they were seeing. As she watched, they stopped at the foot of the statue of one of the great Boer generals astride his horse. *Those old guys were pretty shrewd*, thought Marcia, *to divide the seat of government between the three major cities: the legislative in Capetown, the judicial in Bloemfontein, and the administrative here in Pretoria. I'm not sure I'd want to be in Anna Retief's shoes if she has to move households between here and Capetown twice a year.* The excited chatter of the school children caught her attention again, and she watched them, smiling at their enthusiasm.

An hour and a half later she was back at the Union Buildings, just in time to see Pieter and Dirk emerging from a side entrance, deep in discussion. She watched them stand outside the door for a few minutes, then Pieter saw her and waved to let her know he was coming.

In a few minutes he jumped in behind the wheel as Dirk walked off toward the parking lot.

"Dirk is going to pick up Anna at her sister's and meet us for dinner at the Blue Lagoon. Is that all right?"

"Sure, Pieter. That sounds great. Did you have a good meeting with the minister?"

"Well, it was interesting to say the least. I'll tell you about it when we get to the restaurant."

The Blue Lagoon was one of those modern atmospheric restaurants that had sprung up all over South Africa in the last decade. The dim lighting, dark wood, candles, and tinkling piano in the background all set the mood. Immaculately dressed Indians with Sikh headdresses served tables, while black busboys in white shorts and shirts cleared them. But the guests and manager who greeted and seated them were white. The manager could speak both English and Afrikaans fluently to satisfy whatever side of the political aisle his many distinguished patrons might come from.

Dirk and Anna arrived shortly after Piet and Marcia did, and they were ushered to a quiet corner far from the piano, at Dirk's request.

There was the usual joshing and small talk as they ordered their meal, but as soon as the waiter left, Dirk's face took on a thoughtful expression. "As I was saying, Pieter, this could have serious political repercussions, and we'll have to think it over carefully."

Then remembering that the ladies hadn't been present at the afternoon's session with the Minister of Education, he apologized. "Sorry, my dears, I guess I should fill in the picture."

He leaned forward, folding his hands on the gleaming white cloth in front of him, pushing the unused ash tray aside to make room. "The Minister of Education explained today that the discontent in the high schools in Soweto is far deeper than it seems on the surface. In fact, they have evidence that it is being instigated by communist infiltrators."

"What are they upset about, Dirk? They have more schools than ever out there for blacks now," Anna said.

"Indeed they do, but these commies are very clever. They're telling the kids that by studying in

Afrikaans they are getting an inferior education. You know that we've gradually required that half their subjects in high school be taught in Afrikaans and the other half in English. A policy that simply goes along with our bilingual country."

"What's wrong with that?" Anna asked. "Our kids are all bilingual. I'm sure Geoff can speak as fluently in Afrikaans as he can in English."

"Of course he learned his Afrikaans at home from Piet and Ouma," interjected Marcia.

But Dirk had warmed to his subject. "Lots of English kids can hardly pass their Afrikaans matric after taking it as a subject for thirteen years. But that's just why the Department of Education is insisting that we beef up Afrikaans studies all across the board. If we don't, our language and our Afrikaans culture with it will gradually disappear."

"Haven't the black kids had to take Afrikaans in school all along?" queried Anna. "Why should it be such a problem now?"

Dirk responded, lowering his voice so that they had to strain to hear him, "The trouble is the blacks aren't passing their matriculation exams, so they're blaming it on the language. They claim that they can't learn arithmetic and science in a language they don't know well. In fact, they complain that the teachers who teach these subjects don't know Afrikaans well enough to teach in it."

"But they've had years to learn Afrikaans; this law has been on the books for a long time," Piet interjected. "Why haven't those black teachers learned the language? They've learned English well enough to teach. I just see it as political resistance. They think this is one way to thwart the Nationalist party."

"But what do you fellows have to do with it?" Marcia asked.

"The minister called us in today because they are having to deal with a possible demonstration, not only in Soweto but Capetown, Port Elizabeth, and other places. These kids seem to be getting instruction from some central source. So far the police have kept order, and I don't think they'll let it get out of hand. But we're getting a lot of pressure from the liberals to change the language requirements and to let the students write their subjects in English if they want to."

"What does that mean to your campaign, Dirk?" Anna asked.

"The minister wants me to use my influence in my constituency to back him. He doesn't want to give in — and I think he's right."

"If we back down on this, it'll just encourage them to put pressure on us somewhere else," Piet remarked. "We've got to maintain our language if we are going to retain our Afrikaans culture in this country. And if all the leadership is Afrikaans speaking, then the educated blacks better be, too."

Dirk sat silent for a moment, tracing a pattern on the candlelit cloth with his fork. "I'm in full agreement with Van Heerden. My only problem is the timing."

"You mean because of the elections?" Anna sounded anxious, as though the implications had suddenly become clear.

"Yes. If for some reason we can't hold this thing—if it should explode out in Soweto or any other black area—people will back off. No one wants violence or bad press overseas."

The whole thing is so cold-bloodedly political, thought Marcia as she listened to Dirk's arguments. *What if these students really are failing because they can't understand what their teachers are saying? How would I feel if Gary and Tim had to learn their algebra in French or German?* She wanted to ask the questions, but she didn't dare. Instead, she listened as Dirk went on explaining the dilemma he was facing.

"People are very concerned about maintaining the status quo. If something should go wrong, then anyone who spoke out for a strong position could suffer from the backlash. I sure wish this weren't happening just now."

Pieter pulled at his beard in a way that Marcia knew was characteristic when he was troubled. "I think Van Heerden is overestimating those kids," he said. "They don't have the means to organize a massive demonstration—they don't have the leadership or communications. With our forces so visible out there in Soweto now, I'm sure it's cooling them down in a hurry. They have armored troop carriers stationed at strategic points in Soweto. That should be intimidating enough to scare them off from taking any action.

"Have the students actually done anything yet?" Marcia questioned.

"Not much," Dirk replied. "Some of the schools have had classes disrupted by students standing around on the grounds refusing to go to class. Of course they're just cutting off their own noses to spite their faces.

"They'll never pass their matric that way. This kind of spasmodic rebellion has been going on for weeks, and it hasn't amounted to much. I don't think it will, and I think a word from me in my campaign would just prove my determination to keep this law in effect." Dirk leaned back as though he'd made his decision.

Pieter agreed. "Ya, you're probably right. Giving Van Heerden some public backing will put you in the party's good graces, and probably won't hurt your votes either." Then, glancing up, he grinned. "Hey, here's our dinner. Let's not spoil it worrying about something that'll probably never happen."

On the way home in the starlit night Marcia and Pieter managed to avoid further shop talk. It was cozy and intimate in the darkness of the car. Marcia sat close to Pieter, who drove with his arm around her, as he had so often when they were first married, her hand resting on his thigh.

The music on the radio set a nostalgic mood as they rode through the blackness. There were few cars at this time of the night, and Marcia felt they could have been hundreds of miles from home.

"Remember how we used to drive at night when the kids were little?" she murmured sleepily, dropping her head on Piet's shoulder to get more comfortable.

"Do you want to put your head on my lap and go to sleep?" he asked.

"No, I'm not really sleepy. It's just so relaxing to

ride like this with you. We haven't taken a trip, just the two of us, for a long time."

"Maybe after the elections we could leave the boys with Ouma and go down to Durban for a week."

"Try and leave them behind," Marcia said, laughing, "if they know we're going to the ocean. We'd probably end up with a few *extra* kids — only now it would be girlfriends instead of boyfriends."

"That couldn't be any worse than that scrawny little kid Geoff tried to stowaway with us when he was about eight or nine. What was his name, anyway?"

"Oh you mean Johannes Boshoff, the one who lived with his granny a few blocks from us."

"Ya. Why was it Geoff was so determined to bring him along? Didn't he even pack a suitcase for him?"

"It was something about his parents being divorced. I think there was a custody suit and Johannes was going to have to move in with his dad and he didn't want to go."

"I sure remember the time I had with Geoff," Piet said with a chuckle. "We had hours of 'man-to-man' talks while I tried to explain that we couldn't just take Johannes along without his parents' permission."

"He was determined all right. I'll never forget finding Johannes sleeping under the bed in Geoff's room the night before we left. Those two really thought they could get away with stowing Johannes in the back of the station wagon until we were too far away from home to turn back."

"Geoff just couldn't understand why we wouldn't help his friend who was so unhappy."

"I guess that's still his problem," Marcia remarked thoughtfully. "Only now his friends are 20 million blacks. . . ." Realizing what she'd just said, Marcia could have bitten her tongue. Piet didn't reply but his deep sigh betrayed the hurt he seldom allowed to surface.

They rode the rest of the way home in silence, the atmosphere heavy with the realities of a problem neither knew how to solve.

As they unlocked the front door and stepped into the hallway, they could hear Geoff on the phone in the den. His voice sounded agitated, though they couldn't make out what he was saying.

"I wonder who's calling at this hour?" Pieter ventured.

Marcia started down the hall toward the bedroom when Geoff burst out of the den with such a look of anger and horror on his face that Marcia instinctively cried out, "Geoff, what's the matter?"

Geoff stopped as though he was trying to gather himself together. Then he shouted at them, "What's the matter? It's your fault! I begged you not to call the police. But no, you wouldn't listen. You were afraid you might have lost one of your earrings or a shirt! You *had* to call the police. Well, I hope you're happy. Those police you called have just killed Jacob!"

ELEVEN
The Confession

Marcia and Pieter stood in stunned silence as Geoff hurled his accusations.

"You didn't have to call the police! I told you, Mother, that Jacob was desperate because he needed money for rent." Then turning to his dad, Geoff's voice grew cold and bitter. "Did you know your precious police force is so trigger happy?"

"How dare you accuse us of being at fault?" Pieter retorted. "I did what every decent, law abiding citizen would do. You're so overwrought you can't think straight. I don't want to hear any more accusations."

"Let him talk, Piet," Marcia pleaded, close to tears. She looked at Geoff. "Tell us what happened. How did you learn about this?"

Geoff took a deep breath and swallowed hard; Marcia could tell he was trying to hold back the tears. When he spoke she could hear the strain in his voice. "Thandi just called me from the hospital. Some neighbors who saw the shooting came to the house to tell her about it. They didn't know if Jacob was injured or dead. When she got to Baragwanath, she learned he'd been killed."

"Oh, Geoff, I'm so sorry! I never wanted anything like this to happen," Marcia cried.

Pieter stood unmoved. "Marcia, don't blame yourself. We had nothing to do with this accident."

"Accident?" Geoff bolted forward to look accusingly at his father. "You call shooting a boy in the back an accident? It's cold-blooded murder!"

"And just how did Jacob get shot in the back if he wasn't running from the police? Any policeman in the world would be justified in stopping a criminal from running away."

Geoff shook his head in disgust. "That isn't exactly how it happened. Jacob was in the house when he saw the police stop out in front. He didn't want his mother to see them take him away. She's in a lot of pain. He knew she would be frantic. So he told Thandi to go out and meet them and tell them he was at the corner shop. Meanwhile he ran out the back door and tried to climb over the back fence to get to the store before they did. He knew he'd be better off giving himself up, but he didn't want his mother shamed by seeing what was happening."

"Sounds like a likely story to me," Pieter blurted out. "She'd find out eventually."

"She's dying, Dad—but then *you* wouldn't care.

Geoff's voice was harsh with sarcasm. "They're just natives anyway, and natives don't have feelings like we do, do they?"

"That's quite enough," Pieter shouted. "You don't have to be insulting as well as disloyal."

"Let him finish, Pieter," Marcia said, trying to calm them both. "What happened then, Geoff?"

"Thandi went out and asked the police what they wanted. She told them where Jacob was. She asked them not to go into the house since her mother was very sick. But they wouldn't listen. Two pushed their way past her into the house, while a third went around to check the back. He must have seen Jacob climbing over the fence, for he called the others and they started after him."

"Thandi didn't see what happened. She went back to her mother's room and tried to explain the shouting and noise as just part of a raid. She didn't mention Jacob's involvement, but she doesn't know if her mother believed her."

"After a few minutes one of the neighbors came back to the house to call Thandi. She said Jacob had cut through her yard and run toward the shop. The police van came screeching around the corner—and one of the officers aimed through the window and hit Jacob."

"Oh, my God," Marcia said, shocked. Then she hid her face in her hands.

Geoff continued, his voice cold and restrained as though the telling had given him added control. "The police picked Jacob up and put him in the back of the van and sped off. The neighbor didn't know how seriously Jacob had been hurt. Thandi quickly went to Baragwanath because she knew they would take him there."

Geoff's voice faltered. "She went from office to office, ward to ward, for three hours before she finally traced him to the morgue. He was dead on arrival. They won't even let her see his body until the paperwork is cleared."

Geoff stared for a moment into his father's ashen face. "Is this what your party is after, Father? We keep these people controlled, living on the poverty line, registered and in their place so we can protect our comfortable way of life. And when they step out of line, we have no heart left. We don't dare offer a compassionate response, for it would begin to unravel the system. And then, horrors of horrors, one of our daughters might perform the ultimate sin and marry a black man!"

By now Geoff's voice was raised in anger. "Well, what if one of your sons married a black girl? Your system might work with bullets to stop people, but it can't stop emotions. What would you say if I told you I loved Thandi Ngubane, and that I would do anything I could to marry her? How would your political friends —"

Pieter lunged forward and struck a blow to Geoff's jaw that spun him back against the wall. Blood streamed down his chin and onto his white shirt. Marcia screamed and threw herself against Pieter.

"Stop it! Stop it, both of you! You don't know what you're doing or saying." But Pieter looked past her in a blaze of revulsion at his son, who was slumped against the wall, holding his bleeding face.

"So that's what's behind all this sentimentality about rights and fairness and justice. Just a case of the hots for a little black tart, who has let you know she's available," Pieter said scornfully.

Geoff stared woodenly at his father, holding his hand over his bleeding mouth.

"I brought you up as a decent, law-abiding Afrikaaner," Pieter continued in a hard voice. "But you had to get messed up with those liberals over at Wits and the cheeky blacks they hob-nob with. They don't care about what happens to this country. Well, if that's the life-style you've chosen, I want no part of it. Get out! Go make your way with your so-called friends. But I don't want to see you back in this house again. Not until you break off all contacts with your liberal friends and your black tart!"

Geoff straightened up and wiped his bloody hand on his pants. "She's no tart," he said coldly. "She's a fine, educated, decent girl—"

"Shut up!" Pieter broke in, his voice fierce. "Don't bother trying to explain this. I don't want to hear any more! I've told you what I want, and that's you out of this house—now!" He stalked down the hall into the bedroom, slamming the door behind him.

Marcia sank into a chair in the den, covering her face with her hands as if to blot out the nightmare. Geoff walked past her without a word. She could hear him in his room, opening and closing drawers. Then she heard the sound of his footsteps walking down the hall and the front door slamming behind him.

TWELVE

The Question

The shrill sound of the alarm broke into Marcia's troubled sleep. It seemed like she had just fallen asleep. When she finally went to bed she had lain awake for hours, holding herself rigidly on her side of the bed, trying not to disturb Piet. She had known by his heavy breathing that he was asleep, but his deep sighs and restless tossing had been signs that his anger continued to torment him.

Now Marcia watched through half-closed eyes as Piet got ready for the day. She couldn't let him leave for work without saying something, but what? What was there to say? His anger over Geoff's treachery seemed to enfold her, too.

Piet glanced over at the bed and saw that Marcia was awake. He stood for a moment, looking down at her. Finally he asked, "When did you come to bed last night?"

"Oh, about three I guess. After Geoff left the

house I just sat there going over that scene again and again." She sat up in bed and hid her face in her hands. "How I wish I could have done something to stop you two!"

Piet sat on the edge of the bed and patted her shoulder. But when he spoke she knew the pain in his voice was not for her grief. "You couldn't have stopped us," he said. "Geoff has been asking for this for months. I don't understand what's going on in his mind to do this to us. Especially now!"

"But what's going to happen to him? We can't let him go like this — no matter what he's done, he's our son."

"Marcia, I meant what I said. He's going to have to chose between that girl and us. He can't have it both ways."

"But Piet —"

"Look, this is hard enough without having to buck you, too. Geoff's not just ruining his own life. He could destroy my whole career if this gets out."

He stood up, pulled his jacket on, and went to the door. "He's better off away from this house until he comes to his senses."

"What do you want me to tell Ouma and the boys?" Marcia asked, forcing her voice to remain calm.

"Just tell them he's studying with friends. He's probably moved in with one of his liberal buddies by now."

For the next few days Pieter and Marcia avoided talking about Geoff's revelation. When the boys and Ouma questioned where Geoff had gone, they explained he moved in with a friend for a while because he'd be able to study better with less interruptions.

"Boy, that Geoff sure gets a lot of favors around here," an envious Tim commented. "Sure wish I was twenty-one."

Marcia just tousled his blond curly hair lovingly, thankful that for the time being his greatest problems were blowouts on his bike tires and keeping his growling stomach happy.

Underneath her surface calm, however, Marcia was battling a war with no solution. Guilt was gnawing at her heart—guilt that she had contributed to Geoff's involvement. If she had encouraged him to go to an Afrikaans university like Pieter had wanted, this whole thing probably never would have happened.

But then she would swing into periods of depression thinking of the Ngubane family and Jacob. Hadn't he really been an innocent victim? Shouldn't he have been allowed to move back home with his mother without the danger of arrest? And if he had earned enough money to care for his mother and pay the bills, would he ever have attempted to rob them?

Were there answers anywhere? Pieter and Dirk were so sure the whole apartheid system was the only protection for not only the Afrikaans people but all peoples of South Africa. And it sounded so right when they explained it.

But more and more in recent weeks doubts had overwhelmed her. The facts were there: how could it be fair that 16 million blacks were kept in a second-class situation so that 4 million whites could live the way they wanted to? What was the right answer?

Recently Marcia had begun analyzing things from a religious perspective. She'd always considered herself a Christian. After all, South Africa was considered a Christian nation. Almost everyone belonged to a church, even though many didn't go often. She had been like that. It was only since she'd been attending Ruth's Bible study that she'd realized "Christian" meant something else. It wasn't the same as being a South African because you lived in South Africa, or even Afrikaans because you were born into an Afrikaans family.

Ruth had explained it this way: "God created us all, but we're not automatically born into God's family. That's a deliberate choice—when we accept his Son as our Savior, we become God's adopted children."

She'd explained what the Bible said about being "born again" over and over in the class. Most of the gals were in the same position Marcia was. If someone were to ask them if they were Christians, they would automatically say yes. They were all good Methodists or Presbyterians or Anglicans. But ask them if they had become a member of the "family of God" by confessing their sins and making Jesus Lord of their lives, and they would just shake their heads.

Yet sometime in the past few months Marcia had crossed that line; she'd made the decision to become God's child in a personal and real sense. The Bible had become increasingly more meaningful to her as she'd begun to realize that its teachings were personal instructions for her day-by-day life. And now her doubts and questions about race and politics seemed to stem back to that decision.

She hadn't been able to explain her new faith to Pieter yet. Ruth had told her that she should pray for him and put her faith into practice. Then at the right opportunity she'd be able to tell him about her own experience.

So far in their studies they had not discussed political issues such as she was grappling with. But she was finding her whole value system being affected. Surely the Bible would throw some light on the ethics of apartheid. Did it give guidance about interracial marriages? Was there anything in the Bible about maintaining racial separation or about protecting traditional values and ways of life?

As Marcia got ready for her weekly Bible study, which was to take place that morning, she decided she would have to talk to Ruth about the whole horrible mess. She hadn't felt free to share it before. She'd felt protective of her family and, frankly, somewhat embarrassed that she even had such problems.

But this morning she decided to go to Ruth's early. She needed somebody to talk to, somebody she could level with. Everything was getting too complicated, and she needed some answers.

I'll run over to Ruth's now, she thought. *We can chat before the others get there. I need someone to give me some advice.*

She finished getting ready, then called out to

Angeline in the kitchen, "Tell Ouma I've gone over to Bannister's for my Bible study." And she was out the door and down the driveway.

The street was fairly deserted. Children didn't get out of school until early afternoon and mothers used the morning for shopping, bridge, and clubs. Most houses along this street were cared for by black servants. Marcia saw Paula, the girl who worked for her neighbor on the right, shouting across the fence to one of the black servants hanging up clothes in the next yard. *I wonder what her mistress would think if she knew how much time they spend talking while she's away at work?* thought Marcia. She recalled the fright Paula had given her a few months ago. . . .

Marcia had been sitting on the patio reading the paper when she heard a hoarse whisper coming from the other side of the hedge dividing the property from their neighbors.

"*Nkosikazi, nkosikazi,* help me."

Marcia had dropped her paper and rushed over to the hedge. When she pushed the prickly branches aside, she could barely see Paula, who was pregnant, doubled over in pain.

"What's the matter, Paula?"

"Something's happened, *Nkosikazi.* Come and help me," the girl groaned.

Marcia knew that Paula's employers were both working and that she was alone in the house, so she had rushed over to see what she could do.

By the time she'd reached the *ikhaya,* a back room attached to most white South Africans' homes where the servants were quartered, Paula was lying on the ground, writhing in pain.

Marcia had knelt down beside the girl, and she remembered the terror in her dark eyes. "Where is the pain, Paula? Did you fall down?"

"No, Nkosikazi. There is something happening—something is coming out. Look."

As she lifted her skirt, Marcia had recoiled in horror. The girl was delivering a still-born fetus!

"Don't move. Stay right there, Paula. I'll have to call the doctor."

It had seemed like hours before she got through to her own family doctor. She knew he didn't take black patients, but who did? Where could she go for help? Were there black ambulances that would pick up black patients? Just recently she'd read about an accident where a black man had been hit by a car in a white residential area, and the ambulance that arrived at the scene refused to take him to the hospital because it was for whites only. The man had died.

"Dr. Cronje, this is Marcia Steyn, she'd gasped, the words tumbling over each other. "I don't know what to do. My neighbor's girl is having a baby."

"Just a moment, Mrs. Steyn. Did you say your neighbor's daughter?"

"No, not her daughter, her servant girl. She's lying on the ground groaning. What should I do?"

"Well, Mrs. Steyn, you could probably let nature take its course. These native girls generally have their babies a lot easier than white women do."

"But I think the baby is dead, Dr. Cronje."

"You could take her to the General Hospital.

They have a Bantu clinic in the rear where they handle emergency cases for people in the area. Just put her in your car and take her over there."

Marcia had returned to the backyard where Paula was lying on the grass. The pain had evidently subsided, but she shook with fear.

"Do you think you could get up and walk to my car if I bring it around to the driveway? The doctor says I should take you to the hospital."

Mutely Paula had nodded, and Marcia raced back home, returning with the car in a few seconds. *This is crazy*, she thought. *How will I get her out here to the driveway?*

But Paula was inching along the hedge toward her. Marcia jumped out to open the door and help her get in.

"Wait, Paula. I have a blanket in the trunk. I'll cover the seat so you won't get it . . . so you can lie on it."

Suddenly Paula had doubled over in pain again, and Marcia had steadied her with her hand as she leaned against the car. A muffled groan had escaped her lips, and beads of perspiration stood on her broad forehead. Her maid's cap, which her employer insisted she wear to match her pink striped uniform, was sitting awry on her head, giving her the appearance of a drunk. She was barefoot, having lost her sandals on the grass where she had fallen.

"Come, girl," Marcia said. "Let's get into the car, and get you to the hospital. Marcia recalled how she had tried to be gentle as she helped Paula into the car, in spite of the fact that her knees were shaking from fright, too. She had wanted to get Paula to that hospital before it was too late.

The ride had taken almost fifteen minutes, and Marcia had felt a wash of relief when she saw the five-story brick building looming ahead, its spacious lawns giving it an inviting look. Usually she parked the car on the great curved driveway along the front of the building, but the doctor had said to take Paula around to the back.

Marcia had noticed a service entrance to the kitchen, which was a separate building to one side. She saw no sign of the Bantu clinic, so she leaned out the window to ask a nearby worker. "I have a sick black girl here; where do I take her?"

"Right around to the other side, madam. You'll see a low gray building with a sign for the Bantu Clinic on it."

Gratefully, Marcia had pulled up to the building and raced up the steps to the reception desk. Two young white orderlies about Geoff's age were sharing a joke, tilting their chairs back against the wall.

Breathless, Marcia interrupted their laughter. "I have a sick black girl in the car. She needs attention right away."

"Lady, we only take emergencies here. If she's sick, she should go out to Baragwanath in Soweto."

"But she's delivering a baby!"

"Oh, well, in that case, tell her to come in."

Marcia had stared at the young Afrikaaner in disbelief. "What are you talking about? The baby is already partially delivered. She can't walk in here by herself! Don't you have a stretcher?"

Seeing her anger, the orderly roused himself from his chair and sent the other one off to get a wheelchair. "OK, OK, lady, we'll get her—but these natives are tough. You'll just spoil her with such soft treatment."

That had been months ago, and Marcia had never heard how the actual delivery had gone. She just knew that after a few days she'd seen Paula back in the yard hanging up clothes and shouting over the fence to someone as though nothing had ever happened. In fact, her neighbor, Marie Schuster, didn't know anything about the delivery either; she had not even known that Paula was pregnant.

How can we live so close to people and not know the first thing about them? Marcia mused as she thought over the incident again. *It's as though we are in two different worlds with only one point of contact: when they work for us washing our dishes or cutting our grass.*

This was Marcia's frame of mind when she walked into Ruth's front hall. She was glad to see her alone.

"How nice you came by early, Marcia. How are things going?" Ruth stopped to give her friend a careful scrutiny. "You look as though you could use some sleep. Haven't you been feeling well?"

Beckoning Marcia into the lounge, Ruth dropped into a large beige overstuffed chair near the window while Marcia chose a footstool at her feet. Ruth was short and petite, with natural blonde hair that curled impishly around her face.

She wasn't beautiful; her sensitive skin burned at the first touch of sun, often leaving it red and dry. But she had a delightful sense of humor and an ability to show interest and concern to whomever she met. It wasn't a put-on; she really did care. And as a result, her phone rang constantly as women called for advice or just a listening ear.

"Well, what's up, friend? Is Geoff in difficulty again?" Ruth asked her.

"It's more than Geoff, Ruth. It's Geoff and Pieter . . . and me. I'm so confused. I wonder if even the Bible has an answer for this one."

Ruth just listened without comment as Marcia spilled out her story—going back to the student demonstration at Wits in which Geoff was arrested, then telling how she found the letter from Thandi, and finally describing the conclusion—Jacob's appalling death.

When Marcia finished, Ruth sat silent for a moment, showing neither surprise nor condemnation on her gentle face. Then she leaned forward and put her hand on Marcia's. "Would you like me to pray, Marcia?"

"Oh yes, I've been trying on my own, but it would be so good to have someone else pray for me. I've really been so alone in this," and she pulled a handkerchief out of her pocket to dab at the tears which came unbidden.

"Dear Father," Ruth began, "you see the confusion and heartbreak your child is going through. You know there are no easy answers to this problem, Lord. So many South African Christians are confused and riddled with guilt these days. We don't know how you're going to heal this land and break down the barriers between whites and blacks.

"But, Lord, I pray that you'll give Marcia peace of heart. You know she loves Pieter and Geoff, and it's tearing her apart to see them hurt each other. Help them to be able to forgive each other and to be able to talk this out. Comfort Geoff as he's separated from his family and in his hopeless love for this black girl.

"Lord, show us what your Word has to say about the terrible hurts in this country. Help us to be willing to search until we know your will. And help us to obey your will when we know what it is. In Jesus' name, amen."

"Thanks," whispered Marcia, dabbing at her eyes again. "I didn't want to go all emotional on you, but it's such a relief to be able to talk and pray with someone."

"I know. I'm just sorry you didn't do it sooner." Then getting to her feet, Ruth said, "Let's go out to the kitchen and get ourselves a cup of tea. My girl is home sick today, so I need to get a few things ready for the Bible study gals. We can talk while I do that."

The aroma of the freshly brewed tea gave Marcia a lift, but she knew it was more than the tea. Ruth exuded a confidence and peace that came from deep within herself—not a confidence in herself, but in Someone much greater.

"You know, Marcia," she was saying as she buttered scones and put them on a plate with a lace paper doilie, "there are no nice pat answers to your problem. Oh, the Bible has a lot to say about justice and fairness, and even about God 'being no respecter of persons.' But then it also tells us to 'obey those in authority over us,' and to 'honor the king,' or whatever the ruler of the nation is called. Here in South Africa those two concepts often clash. I guess that's why so many Christians just stick their heads in the sand and pretend there isn't a problem."

"But shouldn't the church speak up when laws are wrong? It isn't right to separate a family by not letting the wife and children live in the city where the husband and father is working, is it?"

"It wouldn't seem so. In fact, I read that the Dutch Reformed Church condemned migratory labor way back in 1966. But it's sort of a statute on the books that no one pays much attention to."

"You don't really have to go any further than the Golden Rule to know that so many of these laws are unbiblical. Would you want Geoff to earn what you paid Jacob? How would you like to be forced to live in Soweto just because of the color of your skin?"

"I never thought of that before, Ruth."

"Or what if Pieter couldn't get a job in an office because those jobs were only reserved for a black man?"

"But does that mean Geoff is right? That we should demonstrate against the government or even worse, break the laws? That doesn't seem biblical either."

"No, and that's what I mean about no easy answers. We need to sort these things out on a personal basis first. Am I treating the blacks who work for me as a Christian should treat them? The people who would make a difference, of course, are men like Pieter and Dirk. I guess that's why Geoff is so agitated. The power lies in the hands of the leaders, many of whom are Christians. But for political expediency, and just plain selfishness, they hide behind our history.

"But," Ruth stopped arranging scones to look directly into Marcia's troubled eyes, "this isn't solving your personal problems. And I don't know the answers to those, Marcia. You owe love and loyalty to Pieter, and his position in the government could be very influential. When he sees his need for Christ himself, perhaps these issues will take on a different meaning. I guess you have to stand with him, encourage him, and pray lots."

"I've been doing that . . . but what do I do about Geoff?"

"The same thing. You can see he's struggling with these same issues. He feels he must take a public stance even though it costs him his education and even his family. What do you really think about what he's doing, Marcia?"

"I . . . I guess he's doing what he believes he should, except . . . except I don't think I could face it if he got more deeply involved with Thandi. Do you think that's right?"

"That's not for me to say, Marcia. The Bible doesn't speak for or against interracial marriages, so I don't suppose we should. I do know it would be a pretty tough marriage to maintain in this society, even if it were allowed. Where would they live? In the colored area where people are neither black nor white? What kind of life would their children have?"

"They'd never make it here. They'd have to go to Swaziland or some other African country. They could never come back home."

"But, Marcia, if Geoff did go through with it, could you still love him and let him know you understood?"

Marcia was silent for a long time, then she answered softly, "I'd have to work through that one, Ruth. But I understand what you're saying. I've got to be willing to accept Geoff's position and let him know I love him. But how will I ever bring his father and him together again?"

"That may take awhile, Marcia," Ruth said looking at her with compassion. "It may just be something you'll have to live with—and pray about. But God can change their hearts and effect reconciliation. I've seen it happen in other people's lives. The important thing is that you trust God to work it out and quit feeling guilty about what happened to Jacob. He did break the law, you know, and you can't blame yourself because our police react violently."

Just then, they heard the sound of a car door slamming out in front of the house. Ruth smiled at Marcia. "The others must be arriving," she said.

Marcia impulsively hugged Ruth as she got up

to greet their friends. "You're so good for me, Ruth. I'm not sure just how this is all going to work out, but at least I'm not carrying it all alone anymore."

The two smiling women went to stand at the front door, cheerily welcoming the other women as they arrived.

THIRTEEN
The Meeting

"Sure . . . I'm almost positive Pieter is free Friday night. If we can't come, I'll call you back. 'Bye."

As she put the phone down, Marcia wondered what Pieter would say about Ruth's invitation. Coming so soon after their talk before Bible study a few days ago, it seemed almost contrived. But she knew Ruth was not that kind of person.

"Jim met this really sharp young African some time ago who's the personnel manager for blacks at a big firm downtown," Ruth had explained. "He was in a seminar Jim was teaching. They got to talking, and Jim found out this fellow, Philip, is a Christian. We've been thinking about having him over, and this Friday seems like a good time."

For a moment Marcia had wondered what Ruth was talking about. "Isn't that against the law?" she'd asked. But Ruth had assured her it wasn't.

"The law doesn't say anything against having blacks in your home or even for a meal. They just can't sleep in your house overnight, unless they are from outside the city."

She had gone on to explain that she and Jim had decided to ask a few couples over for tea one evening to meet Philip and his wife. "And I thought of you and Pieter, Marcia. After what we talked about the other morning, this might be a good way to get some questions answered. How do you think Pieter would feel about this?"

"I'm not sure what he'd say, Ruth. But then again, he's open-minded about most things. He'd probably listen to what this fellow has to say. Do you think this Philip could answer questions without getting angry or defensive? I'd hate to see an argument break out."

"From what Jim said, this man is very well spoken and knows how to act around whites. Maybe he was around missionaries, I don't know. I asked Jim that myself; I wouldn't want anyone to be embarrassed."

"Well, it sounds as if it would be an interesting evening, anyway," Marcia had remarked noncommittally.

Now Marcia sat back in the recliner, and the blue knitted sweater she'd been working on slipped off her lap to the floor as she stared into space.

Would Pieter go to a mixed social gathering? How would he react when he saw the blacks sitting on the lounge furniture? Never in their married lives had an African sat in their living room or had tea out of their good china!

I wonder if we'd be expected to shake hands!

Marcia recalled seeing pictures of the Prime Minister shaking hands with an African dignitary from another country, so it must be done. But she was sure Pieter had never done it before. *Nor have I*, she realized ruefully.

The more Marcia thought about the possibilities, the less likely it seemed that Piet would go — unless she didn't tell him that Philip was black. If she just told him that Ruth invited them over for a social evening to meet some friends, he would go. And Marcia felt Piet was too much of a gentleman to make a scene once he got there. *Besides*, she went on in her mind, *he would enjoy meeting someone new. Pieter likes people and always finds some common point of interest to keep the conversation going. That is one of his strengths.*

Marcia paused. . . . Would that be deceiving Pieter? She'd always tried to be open and aboveboard with Pieter. That was one of the strengths of their marriage. *But this wouldn't really be a deception*, she rationalized. *I just won't explain everything. After all, I don't know who Ruth has invited. All she told me was that a few other friends would be there.*

Suddenly it became very important to Marcia to meet this educated Christian black man. She had never had contact with that kind of African before; she had only met people like Angeline and Paula. They were decent, cheerful, uncomplicated "children." At least, that's the way she considered them.

Nor did she think Pieter had had contact with any blacks similar to this man Ruth had described. Piet often complained about the messenger boys in his office, or the blacks at the garage who wiped his windshield with a dirty rag and left it streaked and worse than when he drove in. But she doubted he would have had contact with any well-spoken educated Africans.

Well, here's his chance, Marcia determined as she put her knitting away. She'd have to find a way to break it to him gently.

When she approached Pieter about the evening at Ruth's, he didn't seem too interested. "I'm not sure I'll be free Friday. You know how many extra meetings Dirk and I have now," he responded as he dutifully pulled out his pocket diary.

"But we so seldom have time for a social evening. You need to get away from the pressure of the office, Pieter. Dirk doesn't own all your spare time," Marcia urged.

"Well, all right. There's nothing scheduled for that night," he replied, looking in his diary. "But if something comes up the last minute, you'll have to explain to Ruth that my time really isn't my own these days."

All day Friday Marcia felt nervous and apprehensive. She hadn't yet found the right moment to explain the plans for the evening to Pieter. When the phone rang around three o'clock, she almost hoped it would be Pieter saying he wouldn't be home in time to go with her to Ruth's.

But it was just one of Tim's friends wanting to talk with him. "He's not here this weekend, Norman. He and Gary are off with the school for a soccer game in Bloemfontein."

Ruth had called earlier in the morning to check on whether or not she and Pieter were coming. "It should be an interesting evening. Our doctor and his wife are coming, as well as several of Jim's old university friends. We encouraged Philip to bring along another couple from Soweto if he'd like."

Marcia cringed. She hoped this would be an informal, relaxed evening.

She still planned to warn Pieter. If he refused to go, she'd just call Ruth and explain. She'd understand. Maybe if they had time to relax over dinner by themselves, she could find just the right moment to broach the subject. The boys were both gone and, of course, Geoff was not there.

Marcia frowned as she thought of Geoff. They hadn't heard anything from him since he'd flung himself out of the house almost a week ago. Every time the phone rang, her first thought was of him. She assumed that what she'd been telling Ouma and the boys was true — that he was staying with one of his friends from the university. But she wished she knew for sure. She wished she could just talk with him, just to let him know she loved him and that she was trying to understand.

Piet, on the other hand, didn't give any evidence that he was trying to understand at all. Only once since the morning Geoff had left had Piet mentioned his son's name, and then it was to bitterly denounce him. "I will never understand what happened to him, Marcia. I only hope he was so upset the other night, he didn't know what he was saying. If he really is involved with this Ngubane girl, I couldn't do anything to protect him from the law." As he had spoken, Piet's face had looked pained.

Marcia put the thoughts of Geoff to the back of her mind. She'd learned to do that the last few days, knowing that brooding only served to trigger more questions from Ouma and the boys.

She dressed carefully for dinner since they would have to leave for Ruth and Jim's right afterward. She looked at herself in the mirror, noting with satisfaction that her new blue wool dress brought out the color in her blue-gray eyes. Her new short haircut was becoming, though Pieter hadn't even noticed it yet. She smoothed the soft material over her streamlined hips and patted her cheeks to give them a little color as she heard the car in the driveway.

When she saw Piet in the hallway, she could tell he'd had a rough day. There were dark shadows under his eyes, and his face was drawn. He'd jerked his tie loose on the way home and he carried it in one hand, his briefcase in the other.

He greeted her in a tired, preoccupied voice. "Hi. Do I have time for a shower before dinner?"

Marcia wanted to put her arms around his neck and encourage him to relax, but instead she answered cheerfully, "Sure, I'll tell Angeline to hold dinner for fifteen minutes." Then glancing at her watch she added, "But it can't be any longer. We're due at the Bannisters in an hour."

"Oh no," Pieter moaned. "I'd forgotten about that. I brought home a briefcase full of reading."

"But Piet, we did say we were going. You wrote it in your diary."

"I remember now. I guess I can do the reading tomorrow, but I'm sure bushed. It's been one of those beastly days at the office with one meeting after another." Then looking at Marcia's troubled face, his voice softened. "I'm sorry, Marcia. This night out means a lot to you. I shouldn't be such an old stick-in-the-mud."

She gave him a wan smile. "You need the night out, too, to get your mind off that all-consuming campaign."

As she turned to go into the kitchen, she heard someone speaking with Angeline. Ouma was back from her shopping spree with her friends. Marcia felt a momentary disappointment as she realized there would be no cozy tête-a-tête with Pieter over dinner.

No matter. She'd had her chance to cancel a few moments ago, and she hadn't taken it. Perhaps the best thing was to brave it out and go to Ruth's "mixed party" without saying anything to Pieter, and face the consequences afterwards.

There were several cars in the driveway when Marcia and Pieter walked up to the verandah of Ruth's house. The high veld night was crisp and clear, and Marcia shivered in her jacket, burrowing her chin into the collar to keep the wind from blowing in.

"Wonder who else is here?" Pieter said as he pressed the doorbell.

"I think some of Jim's university friends will be here," Marcia murmured.

As the door swung open, Jim stood in the hall to greet them. His face lit up in a warm smile as he saw Marcia and Pieter. Jim had been a rugby player in his youth. He was an avid jogger, and his muscular body retained its youthful lines even in the bulky turtleneck sweater he wore. He kept his sandy colored hair cut short to manage the unruly curls that he couldn't control any other way. His heavy eyebrows gave his sparkling brown eyes a quizzical look, and his full beard sprinkled with gray intensified the impression of a mischievous youthful Santa Claus.

"So glad you folks could come," he greeted them buoyantly as he shut the door behind them and turned to take their coats. "I'll hang these up, you just go on in. Ruth will introduce you."

Pieter's hand was on Marcia's arm as they went into the living room. For one fleeting moment Marcia wanted to excuse herself to go to the bathroom or fix her hair. Anything to avoid seeing Pieter's face as they walked into the room. Then she felt his hand involuntarily stiffening on her arm, and she thought he was going to turn her around and walk out. She couldn't see his face as he stood half a step behind her, but she could hear him draw in his breath seeking for composure.

Across the room, deep in conversation with one of the other men, was a distinguished-looking black man. He was seated forward on the chair, his knees apart and his long slender hands folded between them. He was slight of build and very dark skinned. Even at this distance Marcia could see that his eyes snapped with intelligence and his thin mouth played with a smile as he spoke. She had never seen an African so relaxed in the company of whites before.

Even as she thought this, he glanced up and saw Ruth leading her newest guests across the room. The African excused himself and gracefully stood to his feet to meet them. He was taller than Marcia had expected, and he was dressed in a gray suit of the latest fashion, his white shirt sporting cuff links that were exposed just the right amount from the jacket sleeves. He was the only man in the room wearing a tie.

If Ruth was nervous about the introductions, she didn't show it. "Pieter and Marcia," she said, smiling, "I want you to meet Philip Mfeka. He's a personnel manager for the Africans at one of the large firms downtown. Jim has met him several times at seminars he's taught."

Marcia smiled and clutched her handbag, wondering if she ought to put her hand out to greet him. But Philip had slipped his right hand into his pocket and merely inclined his head with a gracious gesture to her and then to Pieter, murmuring, "Good evening."

Ruth then took them around the room introducing them to other guests, and the awkward moment passed. *At least that hurdle is over,* thought Marcia, as she sank into a chair next to Dr. Cook's wife. They were soon chatting congenially, discovering they both had sons at the West Valley High School. But she watched Pieter out of the corner of her eye, standing at the farthest end of the room talking with two other men, jangling the coins in his pocket — a sure sign he was tense.

There was an empty seat next to Philip, but no one seemed to make a move toward him. *We're all a little bit nervous. We're acting like tongue-tied teenagers in an awkward situation*, thought Marcia.

But Ruth came in with the tea wagon and pulled it up next to Philip. Once Jim began serving the cups, the atmosphere seemed to liven up a bit; the automatic functions of pouring and sipping and stirring seemed to bring some normalcy to the situation.

She heard Dr. Cook make an effort at conversation with Philip. "Do you have a family?"

"Yes, my wife Miriam is a nurse out at Baragwanath Hospital, and we have three children, a boy and two girls."

"Are they in school?" Cheryl Cook asked as everyone's attention was drawn to the stilted conversation.

"Yes and no." Philip smiled. "My two younger ones are in standards three and five, so they are in school every day. But my oldest boy is supposed to be in high school, only they haven't had classes for several weeks now."

"Oh, I heard something about that," interjected Ruth. "Aren't the students striking about some problem with the teachers?"

"No, it's that Afrikaans issue," Brad Griffith, Jim's former schoolmate, volunteered. "What's really going on in the schools out there Philip?"

Philip hesitated, obviously choosing his words carefully. He answered without raising his voice, that half-smile still playing around his mouth, "The children are very unhappy about the results. I can only tell you what I hear them saying. But the results have been very poor, very poor, the last few years. Certainly they were better when I completed matric twenty years ago."

"But don't you think things are generally better for the Africans now than they used to be?" Cheryl asked, obviously wanting to keep the conversation on a positive note.

Again Philip thought for a moment, weighing his words, knowing his audience could turn hostile very quickly. "Yes, in some ways they are. . . ."

"There's better housing, more people have cars, and there's that new road out to Soweto," Cheryl continued naively.

"Yes, but I think there are greater expectations, and hence more resentment and anger," Philip replied, no longer smiling. "The young people are more frustrated; they just don't see any possibilities for their hopes being realized. Education has been the only door to opportunity for them to get ahead."

"So why are they refusing to go to classes then?" a voice from the back of the room asked.

"Too many are failing. Parents send their children to school at great cost — fees, books, uniforms, bus fare — to say nothing of the fact that the family loses a wage earner." Philip warmed up to his subject as every eye in the room was riveted on him.

"But," he shook his head, "most of them fail the exams. The children blame the system. In fact," he added ruefully, "they've given up on us. They say we older folks have taken everything sitting down for too long, without demanding our rights."

"What in the hell do they want? That we turn the country over to them on a silver platter?" Pieter's angry question burst into the conversation like an explosion. "If they'd spent their time studying instead of agitating, they'd pass their exams like the European kids do."

In the embarrassed silence Marcia saw all eyes turning in disbelief toward Pieter. No matter how strained the conversation might have been, they had all been trying to make a success of this tenuous effort at bridge building. Now the evening was dangling dangerously.

Anger flashed in Pieter's eyes. Suddenly, he turned to leave the room, but Philip's voice rang out with force and clarity. "You asked what they want—what *we* want. Just wait a minute, Mr. Steyn, and I'll tell you."

As though he couldn't believe his ears, Pieter stopped in his tracks as Philip continued, "I want exactly what you want, Mr. Steyn. I want to be able to have a say in who makes the laws that govern me. I want to be able to own my own house and not feel that at the whim of the government I can be thrown out of the city and forced to live in the country where there are no jobs or opportunities. I want to be able to compete in the job market and not have certain jobs closed to me because of my skin color. I want to be able to look into the eyes of the white man next to me and say, 'I'm a man, just like you are. The same God created me, and I have just as much worth as you have.' " For a moment he looked directly into Pieter's face and then he asked softly, "Is that asking too much, Mr. Steyn?"

And just as deliberately, Pieter murmured through clenched teeth, "You'll never get it. Never!" And he strode out of the room without a glance at Marcia.

For a moment there was a hushed silence. Then Jim stood up. "We're sorry, Philip, we didn't bring you here to be embarrassed. I guess we should have known that Pieter wasn't ready for this kind of interaction. He's on Dirk Retief's campaign, and they aren't exactly pro-African."

Someone else broke into the conversation with an innocuous question about the younger children, and soon little groups were conversing among themselves, trying to salvage what was left of the evening.

But for Marcia there was no salvaging. The worst possible scenario had happened. If only she had listened to her hunches and told Pieter about the evening in the first place. She hated to go home, yet she knew she had to.

It was as though Ruth knew what she was thinking, for she came over and put her arm around her shoulders and whispered, "Don't feel you have to stay. I'm so sorry this happened."

As soon as she could, Marcia bade her embarrassed good-byes and slipped out the front door.

Walking back to the house, she looked up at the diamond-studded sky, and the quarter moon etched in velvet that hung above the houses. "Dear God, I have blown it. I have no idea what to do.

Help me to say the right thing now. Help him to understand . . . somehow. Nobody but you can handle this mess."

Marcia fumbled for the key in her purse and let herself into the front door. The house was dark and quiet.

"Pieter," she called softly, not wanting to alert Ouma that she was home. The last thing she wanted now was to have to explain to her.

There was no answer to her call, so she walked softly down the passage to their bedroom and pushed the door open quietly. The room was dark, and when she switched on the table lamp, she saw that the bed was empty.

For a moment she felt a sense of relief. Perhaps she wouldn't have to face Pieter's anger tonight. She could go to bed and be fast asleep when he came home. Maybe by morning she could figure out some way to handle this new crisis.

But that wasn't the pattern in their marriage. They had always been able to air their differences and talk them over. She'd seen other couples build walls of silence and knew how devastating that could be.

She dropped her jacket on the bed and went back to look for Pieter. If he wasn't in the house, she would just wait up for him. *It's time we talked this thing out*, she thought with a tired determination. *Geoff's problem is driving a wedge between us that could become permanent.*

Pieter was nowhere in the house; even the work area in the garage was dark. So Marcia sat in the living room and stared out the window into the yard where the moonlight cast weird shadows onto the lawn. Her eyes riveted on a dark shape near the garden wall. She jerked forward in her chair and could feel her heart pounding as the terrifying thought passed her mind: Pieter — could he have fallen, or . . . ? Then a breeze touched the treetops, changing the shadow's shape, and she sank back relieved. It was just a bush after all.

The clock in the hall struck eleven thirty when Marcia dragged herself wearily to bed. She wished there was someone she could call, someone who could assure her Piet was all right. But she could call no one without revealing the evening's fiasco.

She comforted herself with the thought that Pieter had probably gone back to the office. But when she checked the study on the way to the bedroom, she found his attaché case where he'd dropped it when he came home from work.

As she crawled into bed she doubted she would fall asleep. But the next thing she knew she was jerked to consciousness at the sound of the front door opening. She glanced at the clock next to her bed. It read 1:15. She heard Pieter's soft tread in the passage, and even as he quietly pushed open the door, she called out, "Pieter, is that you? Where have you been?"

Pieter leaned against the doorjamb. She could see the weary slump of his shoulders in the moonlight even before she switched on the bed lamp.

"I was hoping I wouldn't wake you, Marcia," Pieter said apologetically.

"I wasn't really asleep. Where were you? It's after one o'clock."

"I guess I should have called, but I figured you wouldn't be home till late anyway."

Pieter sat on the edge of the bed to pull off his shoes. "I was so angry when I left the Bannisters I just started walking."

"You've been walking for four hours?"

"No, Dirk came by. He was on his way over to drop off some papers, and when he saw me walking, he stopped to pick me up. We've been over at Potgieter's, his campaign manager, working on Dirk's speech for next week."

As Pieter stood up to pull his turtleneck shirt over his head, he glanced over at Marcia's face and saw the hurt in her eyes.

"Hey, I gave you a fright! I'm sorry!" He sat down on the bed next to her and ran his fingers down the side of her face and neck in a gentle caress. "I ruined your whole evening, didn't I? Losing my temper in front of your friends like that."

Marcia could see his jaw tighten as the whole incident came back to his mind. "I'm just so sick of hearing that sob story about blacks wanting the same chance as we have. They haven't proved they could make the grade as far as I'm concerned. Maybe that Philip what's-his-name could, but you can be sure there aren't many like him."

Marcia didn't want to argue. In fact, she wanted to forget the whole sordid evening. But Pieter mistook her silence. "I am sorry about losing my temper like that. It was supposed to be a nice night out for you." He bent over and kissed her to seal his apology. "But you know," he added, as he stood up to finish getting ready for bed, "your friend Ruth should have told you that she had invited a black. You know I wouldn't have gone. It could have had all kinds of repercussions."

"Pieter . . . she did tell me. . . . I–I just didn't know how to tell you before we went," Marcia said hesitantly. Pieter turned to look at her, his face registering his surprise and anger.

"You knew that black fellow was going to be there?"

"Pieter, try to understand." Marcia sat up hugging her knees under the blanket. "I don't blame you for being angry. I should have told you. In fact, I tried. Even at supper tonight I looked for a way. But, you don't make it exactly easy.

"We'll never sort things out with Geoff until we try to understand how the blacks feel. We needed to meet someone like ourselves. I was afraid you wouldn't give yourself a chance if you knew he was going to be there."

Piet pulled his pajamas over his head and sat down on the edge of the bed next to her. He was silent for a moment. "No, I probably wouldn't have gone. Meeting a black like Philip just muddies the waters. What you don't seem to understand, Marcia, is that for me there is no other option."

For a long time after Piet's regular breathing indicated he was sound asleep, Marcia lay staring into the darkness. She could still hear Philip's penetrating question, "Is that asking too much?" And she knew in her heart she had to answer no.

FOURTEEN
The Eavesdropper

"I'm sorry, Mrs. Steyn. I haven't seen Geoff for about a week. But if I run into him on campus, I'll tell him to call you." The voice on the other end of the line was friendly and unguarded.

"Thanks, John. Sorry to bother you, but I thought maybe Geoff was studying with you today," Marcia responded. She put the phone back and sighed. She'd been calling several of Geoff's friends over the past few days with the purpose of leaving a message for him. It was hard not to let them know that she didn't know where he was.

Of course, Wits was so large that Geoff and his friends could miss each other on the campus. But it seemed strange that even his best friends hadn't seen him for almost two weeks either.

I've got to find him and talk with him, Marcia determined. *We're just breaking apart at the seams. Pieter doesn't want to talk about Geoff. It's*

*so unlike him to harden his heart like this. The
boys are asking questions about him, and Ouma
complains all the time about Geoff being away.*

Since the fiasco at the party Friday night, Marcia hadn't been able to face Ruth. Marcia felt totally isolated with her anxiety and guilt.
Depressed and lonely, she threw herself down on
her bed. Thinking over the Friday before, she realized now how foolhardy the plan had been. Pieter
wasn't ready to accept Geoff's political position,
even if he did get to know an intellectual compe-
tent black. It went against all his training and his
loyalties. If he wouldn't listen to his own son, how
could she have expected him to be swayed by an
unknown black man?

All she wanted now was to talk with Geoff, to
get him to come home. She was sure his relationship with Thandi was a passing involvement,
more out of pity than anything else. Surely by now
Geoff had realized his mistake in getting involved
with the black liberals and was just too stubborn
to admit it and come home. If only she knew
where to find him.

Suddenly she sat bolt upright on the bed.

"Of course, why didn't I think of that before?"
She looked at her watch: 12:15. "I should have
time to get down to the African Family Commission office before lunchtime. If Geoff isn't there,
somebody will know how to reach him." She
didn't let herself think that she might run into
Thandi — she wasn't ready to face her quite yet.

Traffic was heavier than she'd expected, and by
the time she found a place to park the car in down-

town Johannesburg it was already one o'clock and the streets were full of lunch-hour shoppers. Well-dressed Africans as well as crowds of whites strolled along the pavements. Marcia was always impressed at the fashionably dressed European girls who seemed to spend most of their salaries on the latest styles. The white matrons on shopping expeditions, looking as though they'd just stepped out of the hair dresser's shop, intermingled with the lunch-hour crowds. Whites and blacks travelled in their own circles of friends, each group walking along, acting as if the other did not exist.

Many blacks congregated on the corners or sat along the curb eating their lunches. A group of cleaning boys in blue uniforms squatted on their haunches throwing dice with great intensity, while crowds of onlookers cheered their favorites. It seemed everyone wanted to get out of the cold buildings and into the warm winter sunshine, and Marcia found her progress slowed by the strolling crowds.

The African Family Commission office was housed in the upper stories of Windsor Towers, an old stone building that had seen better days. She found the ground floor entrance between a tobacco shop, which filled the air with its pungent fragrances, and a Portuguese fruit store, where apples, oranges, and an array of colorful vegetables were displayed on stands on the sidewalk.

Marcia entered the dingy hallway, noticing the faded and cracked blue tiles that covered it, and went to stand in front of the heavy black doors of the elevator. A battered sign indicated the Commission was on the fifth floor. She would have bypassed the questionable luxury of the ancient elevator for the stairway, but decided five floors was more than she cared to climb. She could hear the chains of the ancient car rattling in the shaft long before it settled with a jolt on the ground floor.

A crowd of laughing Africans talking animatedly emerged. In some buildings there were special lifts for blacks, but since there was only one to serve the seven floors of the Windsor Towers, it was, of necessity, integrated.

A tea boy carrying a covered tray got onto the elevator with her. They stood in alternate corners, each lost in thought, ignoring the other. The boy got out on the third floor, and the elevator heaved upwards, leaving her alone in the dingy, faded cab.

Now that Marcia was almost at the Commission, she wondered what she was actually going to say when she faced Geoff. What could she say that hadn't already been said? But perhaps he had come to his senses in the past two weeks. Oh, she prayed that he had, for Pieter certainly hadn't changed his mind.

The fifth floor was quiet and deserted as she stepped into the long, gloomy hall that was painted a dull beige. The only light came through dusty transoms above the office doors. But she could see well enough to read the words on the first door beyond the elevator: "African Family Commission. Walk in."

She turned the knob gingerly and opened the door. The front office was deserted. There were three desks lined up in a row facing the door, and a file cabinet painted dark green stood in one corner near the window. The desks were covered with files and other papers, as though the occupants had left at the ringing of a bell. She had once owned a black Royal typewriter like the one on the back desk, and she mentally calculated its age at about thirty years. A large tattered map of Soweto hung on the wall, with the smudges of many fingerprints on its once glossy vinyl surface.

She presumed the two doors on the left led to other Commission offices. One door stood ajar and she pushed it open, hoping to find someone in the inner office. But it too was deserted. *Strange*, thought Marcia, *that everyone would go out for lunch and leave everything unlocked. It must mean someone is coming back right away.*

For a moment she stood at the window, looking down at the traffic below, wondering if she should wait or just leave a note for Geoff. Suddenly she heard a door opening and someone talking in the front office. She started to step toward the partially opened door, but then she froze. Though the occupant was out of her range of vision she recognized the voice as Geoff's.

She felt a momentary sense of relief — he was all right. There were times during these weeks of silence when her imagination had run wild, and she wondered if he'd left the country or had suffered an accident or been hurt.

She was about to step into the outer office when she heard a woman's voice.

"Geoff, you shouldn't be here during the lunch

hour. Everyone knows it's my day to answer the phone while the rest are out. What will they think if they come back and find you here?"

Marcia stood riveted to the spot. Thandi! She couldn't face the two of them together. How could she get out of there without going through that outer office? Noticing another door behind her, she stepped back gingerly to turn the knob. Locked! She might have known it would be locked during lunch hour. She look frantically around her, but there was no exit — except through that front office.

Just then Geoff and Thandi moved into her line of vision through the partially opened door. They were completely unaware of her presence.

"I don't care about them," she heard Geoff say. Then he added tenderly, "I'm worried about you. I haven't had a chance to talk with you since Jacob's death. How's everything going at home? How's your mother taking it?"

Marcia could barely hear Thandi's reply. "Not very well. In fact, on the day of the funeral I was afraid she wouldn't be able to go to the church. I tried to get her to the doctor, but there were so many relatives and friends around, and so many preparations to take care of, she wouldn't hear of it."

"I wanted to come to the funeral, Thandi, but I knew they wouldn't give me a permit . . . and I guess I was worried that I'd cause you more problems than I have already."

"You haven't caused me problems, Geoff. You've been so helpful. I haven't even had the chance to thank you for the money you sent out. You'll never know how that helped with the expenses."

"I wish it could have been more. I know you had all the burial expenses and extra people to feed for over a week. How did you ever manage?"

Marcia could see Thandi standing in front of the window. She stood still, except for the nervous tracing of her fingers along the paint-flaked window sill.

"I borrowed money from friends to buy the coffin. People gave us gifts — neighbors, friends in the church. One of the men in our church had a big open truck, and we used that to take people to the cemetery."

"Thandi." Marcia could see Geoff as he moved closer to Thandi and put his hand on hers to stop her nervous motions. "I wish I could tell you how sorry I am this happened. If only I could've given Jake the money for the rent myself or been able to explain to my parents. But I just couldn't get through to them."

"Don't blame yourself, Geoff. Jake couldn't handle the Soweto situation, and I couldn't control him either. He would have gotten into trouble sooner or later." Then her voice broke. "I just wish Mother could have been spared this right now. She's gotten so much worse."

Thandi put her hands over her face, and Marcia could see her shoulders shaking as she muffled her sobs.

"What do you mean, gotten worse? What else has happened, Thandi?" Geoff took her by the shoulders and turned her to face him. Even at this distance, Marcia could see the pain in his own eyes as he listened to Thandi.

Frantically Marcia looked around the room once more for some kind of escape. *I don't want to hear this*, she almost cried aloud. But the nightmare played on.

"She's in the hospital." Thandi sighed as she rubbed her tear-stained eyes with the palm of her hand. "The day after the funeral she had a terrible attack of vomiting and pain. She couldn't even get out of bed. Fortunately my uncle from Natal was still there with his car, so he took her to Baragwanath."

"What do the doctors say is the matter?"

Thandi shook her head. "I can't get any answers from anyone. The doctors are never there when I go to visit her, and the nurses won't say."

"Have they helped her at all?"

"No. I'm afraid there's something seriously wrong. She's been sick for so long. Oh, Geoff, I think she's dying."

Marcia watched as Geoff gathered the sobbing girl into his arms and gently held her as she burrowed her face in his shoulder. As long as she lived, Marcia knew she would never forget the sight of the dark head resting against Geoff's bronzed skin, a silhouette of hopelessness and tragedy.

Then she heard Geoff murmur, "Thandi, if only I could do something. If only I could take care of you. You know I love you, don't you?"

Thandi pulled herself erect so she could look into Geoff's face. "Don't even say that. What good does it do?"

Goeff pulled her against him stroking her face as it rested against his shoulder again. "I've been doing a lot of thinking since I left home. Nothing will change here. We're fooling ourselves to think that our demonstrating and organizing will ever get this government to see what they're doing."

Thandi lifted her head, as though to speak, but Geoff just held her tighter. "No, listen to me. I've decided to leave South Africa. I'm not sure just where I'll go — maybe Swaziland or England. I've quit school and have a job. As soon as I've saved enough money we can both go someplace where we can be married. Oh, Thandi, I want to take you away from all these insults and hurts."

Marcia saw a look of incredulous wonderment come over Thandi's face as she looked into Geoff's blue eyes and saw the tenderness and deep concern mirrored there. Before she could answer him, he bent to kiss her, and she responded without hesitation, slipping her arms around his neck and crushing his blond head against hers.

Suddenly, the shrill ringing of the telephone broke into the silence, and Geoff and Thandi sprang apart, terror in their eyes. At that moment a key turned in the door behind Marcia and a young black girl stepped into the room. Before the girl could ask what Marcia was doing in her office, Marcia spun on her heels and leaped into the hall. She fled past the elevator and the laughing lunch-hour crowd getting out of it, and pushed open the door to the stairway. She could hear the clatter of her footsteps on the cement stairs as well as a strange wailing noise which she realized was coming out of her own throat. Halfway down the stairs she stopped her frantic descent and slumped down on the stairs, her head leaning against the grubby cement wall, her legs rubbery and unwilling to hold her up.

Listening to the echo of her own heavy breathing in the musty dark stairwell, she tried to gain her composure. "God, what do I do now? Oh, what a mess!" she wailed into the empty gloom. "What's going to happen now? I don't know what to think anymore. Help me, oh help me." And her sobs reverberated and disappeared into the distance below.

She didn't know how long she sat there, cradling her head on her arms, but gradually a quietness poured over her. It was as though she was being wrapped in a cotton batting to protect her from shock. Her senses were numb, and she rocked back and forth on the cold, cement steps.

Then, after a timeless interval, she pulled herself wearily to her feet and stumbled down the rest of the stairs and out of the building into the brilliant sunshine.

FIFTEEN
The Death Sentence

Marcia knew she was driving the wrong direction, but when she found herself on the Main Reef Road heading west instead of north, Marcia realized this was no accident. Subconsciously her heart was telling her where to go and what to do next.

Mrs. Ngubane. Somehow she had to talk with Thandi's mother. She would know how to persuade Thandi to refuse Geoff's offer. She would see, as only a mother could, that there was no future in their love — only heartache and loneliness and pain. Even if they went to another country, their backgrounds were too dissimilar to ever mesh smoothly.

And she knew that Thandi loved her mother and would listen to her. That was more than she could say for Geoff. The break between them was worse than she had imagined. It seemed incredible that he could even think about leaving South

Africa. What would Pieter do when he learned that Geoff had quit Wits? She couldn't keep it from him for long; the school would report it.

Marcia had never been to Baragwanath Hospital, but she remembered seeing a sign as she turned off from the Main Reef Road right near the first gold mine shaft that had been preserved as a memorial. She had driven a carload of boys to see the shaft when Tim was in Standard Five.

She drove through several miles of mine property, barely noticing the barracks that housed thousands of blacks from all over Africa who came to work in the mines. Most of the land lay barren and windblown, or covered by massive mine dumps.

Marcia started to worry that she had missed the hospital, but then the traffic thickened and she found herself driving along a high stone wall that enclosed several large buildings and smaller prefabs. That must be it!

She knew Baragwanath was a large hospital — she once read it had over a mile of corridors — but she had no idea it covered so much territory. Outside the main gate hundreds of people milled about, standing in lines that stretched for a block, waiting for buses or hailing taxis. A parking lot across the street was filled, but she noticed some cars were driving through the emergency entrance, so she followed them. When the guard saw a white woman at the wheel, he waved her past.

Once inside, Marcia was overwhelmed. It was like a small city of its own. Long barracks-like buildings were connected by sidewalks and covered walkways. Everywhere she saw patients, dressed in gray or blue hospital gowns, lounging on the grass or leaning up against the sunny side of a building.

A black nurse, dressed in a navy cape over her white uniform and a white shoulder-length headgear that framed her face, walked toward her. Marcia stopped the car and leaned out the window.

"Sister, can you tell me where I might find a patient by the name of Ngubane?"

"Go over to the large emergency doors beside that uniformed guard and turn right," she said, pointing to a large building down the road. "As you enter, you'll see the office just around the corner."

An ambulance with its sirens screaming swung past her, and people on the street scattered to avoid being hit. An old man stood at the curb watching the ambulance disappear around the corner. His head was swathed in bandages. His bony finger clutched his oversized pajama pants around his waist to keep from losing them. Marcia wondered if he was reliving his arrival. She waited for him to shuffle painfully across the road in front of her before she drove on to park her car.

Once inside the hospital buildings, she was again reminded of the bedlam at the Bantu Affairs office that she'd visited with Jacob. The walls were lined with hard wooden benches, all of which were filled with people waiting their turn. A woman held a screaming little girl in her arms, while a distraught man tried to calm her. Others sat with their heads resting on their arms; some even slept, sprawled in awkward positions against their neighbors.

There were long lines in front of the desk, and all the clerks behind the counter were black. But it didn't seem to soften the atmosphere. A young woman, dressed in a tight-fitting green pantsuit and wearing bright red lipstick and nail polish, declared angrily to an old woman in front of the counter, "I told you before, I have no one by the name of Simon Nkosi on my records. Go get his identification number if you want to see him." Dismissing her with a scornful look, she shifted her eyes past the woman. "Next?"

The bewildered old woman, tears coursing down her wrinkled cheeks, shook her head, and turned to look helplessly about her. She spoke in one of the Bantu languages so Marcia couldn't understand her words, but she was deeply agitated and gestured hopelessly with her hands to those around her.

As though reading Marcia's thoughts, a young man standing beside her volunteered, "She's looking for her son. The neighbors said he was hit by a car and was brought here. But she's been here three days in a row, and no one can tell her anything."

"Oh, what a shame," uttered Marcia, her heart going out to the old lady. "How will she find him?"

"If he's here, he'll eventually get someone to send a message to her. If he's in the morgue and had his pass on him, they'll contact her. If not . . ." He shrugged his shoulders and grimaced as if to say, "You know how it is out here."

Then, as though remembering his manners, he asked, "Are you looking for someone, madam?"

"Yes . . . a friend. Well, not really a friend, but the mother of someone I know. It's important that I see her. I wonder now if I'll ever find her in all this confusion."

"Oh, don't worry, madam, they are used to helping Europeans. If you go to that office over there and explain what you want, they'll take you to your friend."

Thanking the young man, Marcia hurried through the crowd to the office he had indicated. A middle-aged white woman sat behind the desk, speaking on a phone cradled under her chin while she signed forms brought by one of the clerks. The woman was dressed in a nurse's uniform, a tiny wide-winged cap perched on her graying hair as though ready to take off in flight.

She smiled up at Marcia and said, "I'll be right with you," then gestured to the scarred brown wooden chair in front of the desk. She spoke for a few more moments in what seemed to be fluent Zulu, then put the phone down.

"How can I help you?"

By now Marcia was feeling as though she was asking the impossible. Her fear was beginning to wear off, and the regret of her impetuousness was surfacing. "Well, I . . . I had no idea how difficult it would be to see someone here at Baragwanath. I need to see Mrs. Ngubane, and I heard she was here so . . ." her voice trailed off.

"Oh dear," replied the woman whose name on

her identification badge was Doreen Hayward. "We have lots of Ngubanes here. There are several thousand patients in this hospital on any given day. You wouldn't happen to know this Bantu's first name would you? It would be much easier to find her that way. Or do you know where she lives?"

"Yes, I'm pretty certain her name is Grace, and she lives in Dobsonville. I've b—," Marcia stopped. She almost said she'd been there but thought better of it. The woman nodded and rose to her feet.

"That should help. Come with me, Mrs. . . . ?"

"Steyn, Marcia Steyn."

"Well, Mrs. Steyn, we'll find her records in the other office, and then I'll get someone to take you. You could easily get lost here."

Marcia waited only a few minutes before Mrs. Hayward returned with a manila folder in her hand.

"You may be too late, Mrs. Steyn."

"Oh no." Marcia's hand flew to her throat. "Has she . . . ?"

"No, no, she hasn't died. Not yet. But you do know it's a hopeless case, don't you?" The woman paged through the papers in the file, studying them more carefully. "She's been here as an outpatient over the past two years, but her cancer has now progressed to the place that there's little more we can do. We've put her on medications and are releasing her today."

"How . . . how long does she have?"

Mrs. Hayward looked at the charts again. "Dr.

198

Retief gives the prognosis as two or three months at the outside. The cancer has invaded her liver. She will probably be back in the hospital again in a few weeks. We are so overcrowded that we send people home as long as there's someone to take care of them."

"But this woman doesn't have any income. How will she pay her bill? Her daughter only has a part-time job."

"Well, fortunately they pay next to nothing for hospital care. It costs less than a rand to be admitted, and then everything is free. And we have excellent doctors here, Mrs. Steyn, contrary to what people say. They're the best. Of course they're overworked and our wards are crowded, as you'll see."

"You say that Grace has been discharged. Do you think she's left already?"

"I doubt it. She'll have to find someone to take her home. I don't suppose she's strong enough to take the bus. You say she has a daughter? If her daughter comes to visit her today, she'll probably arrange for her to take a taxi home. We can't provide ambulance service for released patients of course."

A thought struck Marcia. "Would I be able to take her home?"

Mrs. Hayward looked surprised. "That's up to you, I suppose. We have nothing to say about how a discharged patient goes home. But I'm not sure you would be wise going into Soweto alone — especially these days."

"Oh yes, I forgot about the situation out there.

Well, I'll go talk with Grace. Maybe she has already made arrangements."

Marcia followed the young black orderly Mrs. Hayward had assigned to take her to Ward H. She wondered how the nurses ever knew where their patients were, so many of them were outside basking in the afternoon sunshine. She passed two European doctors dressed in white coats deep in conversation, with stethoscopes dangling from their pockets. When they saw her, they nodded a greeting and one asked, "Can I help you?"

"No, thanks. This young man is taking me over to Ward H."

Satisfied that she wasn't lost in this alien place, the doctor turned back to continue his conversation. Marcia suddenly realized that, except for Mrs. Hayward and these two doctors, she was the only white person in sight.

She stopped to let two chattering nurses push a trolley past her. The man on the cart seemed to be unconscious; an intravenous drip attached to his arm was being wheeled along beside him. Marcia wondered if he was coming from surgery. It seemed the nurses had to move their patients long distances from surgery to the wards.

The orderly stopped and directed her to a gray two-story building. "Ward H is in there, madam. The sister in charge will take you to Mrs. Ngubane."

Marcia entered the door and was immediately struck by how cold it was inside. Only a little sunshine penetrated through the small windows of the building. *No wonder everyone who is able gets outside for warmth*, thought Marcia.

A large block H was painted above the first door to her right, and she could see two rows of narrow iron beds lining the length of the gray walls. There was just room for a tiny metal table between them. But the patients in this ward were not out basking in the sunshine. At first glance, Marcia calculated were about twenty women in the ward, most of whom were attached to an intravenous drip. Marcia presumed that many of these patients were probably in the advanced stages of cancer. Most were emaciated and comatose. Anxious friends or relatives stood around their beds; some sat on blankets on the floor, as though settled in for a lengthy stay.

The one nurse on the ward was moving from bed to bed taking temperatures and blood pressures. And if she noticed Marcia standing in the doorway, she didn't let on.

For a moment Marcia thought she recognized Grace in the second bed, and she stepped forward. She had only met her once, but she remembered the round face and high cheek bones, just like Thandi's. That day in Soweto, Grace's head had been covered with a colorful scarf, as was usual for married African women. But this patient's short gray hair was matted and scruffy from tossing on a pillow. She rolled over in the bed, a weak moan coming from her throat, and for a moment she opened her pain-tormented eyes.

Marcia stopped as she realized that it wasn't Grace. As she stood uncertainly near the door, another nurse came by pushing a cart of medications. She seemed almost too young to be qualified, but her perky pleated cap and official badge identifying her as Rose Khumalo verified her status. "Are you looking for someone, madam?" she asked in a soft refined voice.

For a moment Marcia looked into her intelligent and friendly eyes. Her graciousness was like a breath of spring in the cold atmosphere of this seemingly understaffed institution.

"Can you tell me if Mrs. Ngubane, Grace Ngubane, is still here?" Marcia asked.

"Mamma Ngubane? Yes, she's at the far end on the left. She's supposed to go home today, but no one has come for her. Are you her madam?"

"No, I-I know her daughter," Marcia replied quickly. "Uh, how is Grace feeling today?"

Rose shook her head. "She feels a little better when she takes her medications regularly, but she is very weak. Is her daughter coming to take her home?"

Marcia followed behind the nurse as she pushed the squeaking cart up the aisle between the beds. In spite of its drab austerity, it gave Marcia the impression of order. A strong odor of disinfectant permeated the air.

"I don't know. Have you let her know her mother has been discharged?"

"I don't think so, madam. The doctor just signed the discharge sheet when he made his rounds about two hours ago. We just tried to call the office where she works, but they said she had left for the day."

She must have left right after I did, thought

Marcia. Maybe she and Geoff left together. The vision of Thandi in Geoff's arms brought the whole urgency of her visit back to her mind. Grace just had to do something to stop Thandi's relationship with Geoff before it was too late.

But when Marcia saw Grace, her resolve faltered. The woman lay motionless, her breathing labored and shallow. Her eyes were sunken into the dark hollows above her prominent cheekbones, from which the gray flesh sagged. No wonder Thandi was worried. Even without the confirmation of the doctor's prognosis, Marcia would have sensed her mother's life was slipping away.

Touching Grace's arm gently, Rose announced, "Mamma Ngubane, there is a visitor to see you."

An inner strength seemed to turn on as Grace opened her eyes and smiled wanly at the nurse. She lifted her hand in a weak gesture of welcome, and the young nurse clasped it warmly in both of hers for a few seconds. It was evident she loved the older woman — not as a patient, but as a friend.

"Mamma Ngubane goes to my father's church. She's known me since I was a little girl," Rose explained to Marcia.

Marcia stepped closer to the bed, and Grace looked at her with surprise and bewilderment.

"Grace, I'm Mrs. Steyn. You remember when I came to visit you several weeks ago — when Jacob was missing?" As she spoke the words, Marcia momentarily turned her face away as the shocked realization of what she was doing suddenly overcame her. How could she have forgotten about

Jake? How could she come to this dying woman with her own problems—this woman who had just lost her only son. Especially since Marcia was probably at fault for his death! She swallowed hard and turned to look at the woman lying in front of her.

"I'm so sorry about Jacob. Grace . . . I didn't mean for anything like that to happen. I know now he was just trying to help you," she offered.

Rose pulled a bent-up metal chair over to the bed and offered it to Marcia, who sank into it gratefully, fighting for control.

As the two women looked into each other's eyes, compassion bridged the chasm that separated their worlds. Grace's emaciated face could not hide her concern as she saw the anguish of this white woman who had tried to help her family. Grace seemed to sense that this woman was different from the "madams" she had worked for all these years. She was the first white woman who had ever come to her home. And now she had come to the hospital.

When Grace spoke, her voice was so soft that Marcia had to lean over the bed to hear her. "Thank you for coming, *nkosikazi*. It's not your fault about Jake." A tear rolled down her cheek, and she wiped it with the corner of the sheet. "Jake didn't understand about Soweto. He didn't have faith to believe that God would help us. He was angry all the time. I tried to send him back to the country, but he wouldn't go."

"He wanted to stay and work to help you," interjected Marcia reassuringly.

"I know. And you gave him a job so he could stay here. Thank you, *nkosikazi*. I'm so sorry he wasn't a good boy. I always tried to teach my children to be good Christians. My husband was a preacher. Jacob went to church every Sunday when his father was alive, and we taught him about the Lord Jesus. But after Ngubane died, I had to send Jacob away to the country to his granny's because I couldn't keep him with me where I worked. He didn't go to church anymore."

Grace tried to shift to a more comfortable position, and Rose, who continued to hover nearby, rearranged the pillows at her head.

"*Nkosikazi*, I know how bitter and angry Jacob was about the white government in South Africa. The friends he made here in Soweto weren't good for him. They were full of hatred. Every day I prayed that the Lord would fill his heart with love instead of hate, with forgiveness instead of revenge."

She sighed. "But when I spoke of those things to Jacob, he just laughed. He said Christianity is the white man's religion. He didn't expect God to change anything for blacks in South Africa. He said the black people would have to do something themselves. I knew he would get into trouble someday. I was afraid all the time."

"But weren't you angry when the police shot him like that?"

"I was very angry. But as I prayed, God reminded me how much he loves me and that he is powerful. He will punish those unjust officers in his own way. I believe Jacob's life was in God's care. I don't know why God allowed Jacob to be killed." Her voice broke and Rose patted her shoulder sympathetically as Grace drew a deep breath to retain her composure. "But I believe the Bible where it says all things work together for good to those who love God. Maybe someday I'll understand why it happened."

"If only we hadn't called the police," Marcia cried. "Maybe it wouldn't have happened. Can you forgive us?"

With unexpected strength, Grace raised herself up on her elbow and reached her thin hand out to take Marcia's in her own. "There is so much we both have to forgive, *nkosikazi*. But God has forgiven the most because we have done so much to hurt him. If he loves us enough to forgive us, shouldn't we forgive each other?"

Looking into those pain-filled eyes, Marcia felt for the first time she really understood the true meaning of God's forgiveness. Most of her life she had ignored God. She had no room for him in the scheme of her life. Yet how readily he forgave her when she accepted Christ as her Savior and as the Lord of her life.

She looked down at the hitherto unthinkable sight of that frail black hand clasping hers. She placed her other hand over it and patted it gently. "I'm just beginning to understand how much there is to be forgiven," she whispered.

For a moment the two women sat in silence, and then Marcia asked softly, "What are we going to do about our children, about Thandi and Geoff?"

"Hau, hau, hau." Grace shook her head with the characteristic Zulu expression that was a cross between incredulous surprise and disbelief. "Are they now in difficulty, too?"

As gently as she could, Marcia described the scene between Geoff and Thandi in the African Family Commission office. When she'd finished, Grace lay back against the pillows, her eyes closed. For a moment Marcia feared she had fallen unconscious, but then she saw the lips moving.

"My poor child, my poor child. She's losing everything—her brother, her mother, and the young man she loves."

"You don't think she'll agree to go with Geoff, do you?" Marcia asked anxiously.

Grace opened her eyes, "No, *nkosikazi*. We have spoken of this between us. She feared her feelings for your son were growing too strong. She knows such a marriage could never work. Of course, he had never spoken about leaving the country, but I don't think she would agree to that."

"Even when you're . . . I mean, even if she's left alone?"

"I don't think so, *nkosikazi*. But if it will put your mind at ease, I will speak to her. She will listen to me."

Suddenly a white nurse strode over toward Grace's bed, interrupting their conversation in a hard sounding voice with a heavy Afrikaans accent. "Well, my girl," she said imperiously, looking at Grace, "aren't you ready to go home yet? I see the doctor discharged you this morning. Come, come, why aren't you dressed?"

Grace lay back on the pillows wearily, and Rose answered for her. "We've been trying to get hold of her daughter, Sister, but there's no reply."

"Then she can take a taxi. We have other seriously ill patients who need this bed. Can't fool me, my girl. The doctor says you're well enough to go home. You're just trying to show the madam here how sick you are."

Marcia recoiled in horror, and it was all she could do to keep from making a sharp retort. Instead she heard herself say in a cold voice, "I was just going to make arrangements for taking Grace home myself."

"Well, isn't that kind of your madam, Grace? Aren't you a lucky girl." Then turning to Rose she went on, "Make sure this bed is made up as soon as Grace leaves. I have another seriously ill patient out in the hall that should come in here." Then, nodding to Marcia, the woman continued on her rounds.

SIXTEEN
The Riot

In the end, Marcia realized that Rose's suggestion was a good one. Grace was too weak to sit up in the front seat beside her.

"She'll be more comfortable lying on the back-seat, madam," she urged, as she helped Grace out of the wheelchair and into the car that Marcia had pulled up to the end of the walkway.

Somehow it had been important that Grace sit beside her, almost as a defiant gesture for all the world to see that this sickly elderly black woman was her friend, not her servant—someone with whom she had shared a common heartache. And more than that, someone who shared a common faith and a common forgiveness.

She went around to the trunk and pulled out the special travel pillow and blanket she always carried and helped Rose tuck them around Grace. She listened one more time to Rose's careful instructions about the medications for Grace.

"Make sure her daughter understands these have to be given to her right through the night. Tell her I'll be over on my day off to visit and see how Mamma Ngubane is." Then leaning into the car she patted Grace's shoulder and reminded her, "Be sure to direct Mrs. Steyn the back way. There are rumors that the high school students are planning a march today, and you wouldn't want to get caught in that!"

Even with that warning ringing in her ear, Marcia had no fear driving into Soweto on this sunny afternoon. It was as though things finally made sense, at least for her. She saw now that Geoff and Pieter were both wrong. The fighting, rebellious attitude that put Geoff on the outs with everyone only bred trouble for him and heartache for those he loved. And the attitudes of stubborn resistance to change, the unwillingness to see the blacks' point of view, and the determination that might makes right that Pieter and his political friends had, were wrong, too.

There was another way, a third way—the way Grace and she had discovered this afternoon. It was the way of sharing their common problems, of realizing they both felt the same kind of pain when their children suffered, of opening up to each other and forgiving, as Christ had forgiven them.

If we could just start there, she thought, as she drove carefully along the main road that skirted Soweto, where the afternoon traffic was just beginning to build up. *There are so many Christians among the whites and blacks. If we just practiced the simple things that Jesus taught us about love and forgiveness, we could at least start talking to each other like people. We could at least build some bridges for people like Pieter and Dirk to cross.*

She wished she could talk more about this with Grace, but she saw in the rearview mirror that she had dropped off to sleep. The effort to get dressed and to bid her good-byes to the nurses and patients who had become her friends during the stay had taken its toll.

Lost in her own thoughts, Marcia did not notice the sullen stares of the young people who stood in clusters on the street corners. Nor could she understand the bitter shouts that were hurled after her as she drove by. When they reached the Ngubanes' house, Marcia began helping Grace out of the car. A neighbor woman ran up to offer her assistance. Between the two of them, they managed to get Grace into the house and onto the lumpy couch in the front room Marcia had seen the last time she was there.

She could sense the uneasiness of the neighbor whom Grace introduced as Sarah. The woman disappeared into the kitchen and Marcia heard her bustling around the black cast iron stove that the Ngubanes used for both cooking and heating.

Marcia placed the bottles of medication she'd brought from the hospital on the table.

"Rose gave me your medications, Grace. I'll put them here on the table so your daughter will see them all."

Grace started to sit up, but Marcia put her hand on her shoulder. "No, don't get up. You need to rest after all the excitement. And you must stay covered up. It's so cold in here." Marcia realized she herself was chilled to the bone even though she had a wool jacket on. "Do you have another blanket I could put over you?"

"Sarah can get one for me. She knows where they are."

Just then Sarah appeared at the kitchen door, drying her hands on the faded gingham apron she wore over her print house dress and bulky black sweater. "I've cleaned all the ashes, Mamma, but there's no coal in the tin. Do you have some out back?"

Grace shook her head. "I don't keep it outside. It just gets stolen. When Thandi comes, she'll go get some. I'm all right if I just have another blanket."

"I could send my boy to find a coal man to bring you some coal if you give me some money," Sarah offered.

"No, that's a bother. Thandi can get it later."

Marcia listened with a dawning comprehension, then fumbled in her bag for her wallet. Drawing out a five rand note, she handed it to Sarah. "Here, have your boy order two bags of coal. Will that be enough?"

Sarah nodded. "I'll go over home and send him. I'll be right back, Mamma Ngubane."

Marcia sat gingerly on the edge of one of the dining room chairs. Grace was lying back on the couch with her eyes shut, exhausted from the afternoon's exertion. Marcia glanced at her watch.

Four o'clock. She was going to be caught in the afternoon rush hour for sure.

Somehow the idea of being here without a permit didn't bother her. She felt so right about bringing Grace home that she would defend herself in court if she had to. But she needed to get home soon. No one knew where she was. Yet she couldn't leave Grace here alone. . . . She would just have to wait until Sarah returned.

As she sat in the silence of the little house, Marcia listened to the tick of the clock from the bedroom and watched the late afternoon sun casting long shadows across the room. There was a faint smell of smoke in the air. *It probably never disappears between the time the morning fires die down until the afternoon ones are built*, she thought.

Glancing around the room, Marcia was again impressed with its neatness and the efforts that had been made to give it a homey atmosphere. The plastic flowers still stood in a vase on the table, but someone had replaced the doily with an embroidered and carefully mended tablecloth. Some school books were stacked on a small table next to the couch, and a well-worn Bible lay on top of the books. The worn and cracked blue-flowered linoleum, which covered the space between the couch and the table, was shining as though it had recently been waxed. Marcia wondered whether Thandi or relatives who had come for the funeral had done it.

It suddenly occurred to Marcia that coal might not be the only item missing from the Ngubanes' kitchen. She hadn't had a chance to ask Grace, but evidently someone had paid the rent since they were still here. Perhaps that's why there was no money left for coal. . . . What about food?

Marcia tiptoed quietly into the kitchen. The large black stove, gleaming from Sarah's ministrations, was the prominent feature. An empty woodbox stood next to a tin, presumably used for coal, in the corner beside the stove. A small table covered with a plastic red-and-white checked cloth and a kitchen dresser stood on the opposite wall. Through the glass doors Marcia could see an assortment of dishes — but no food.

Feeling like an intruder, she opened the bottom doors. A few tins of spice sat on the top shelf, a half-filled bottle of oil and a third of a five-pound bag of mealie meal. That was all. A tin marked "tea" was empty, as was the sugar bowl.

Had Jacob come home to this after spending his days in her garden and watching her eat on the patio with bowls of fruit and plates of meat and cheese? How had he felt when she'd given him slabs of dry bread and a mug of tea for breakfast, knowing his mother and sister might not even have had that?

If she had known this then, if she had bothered to find out, would she have done things differently? Would she have paid him more?

She heard Sarah's voice outside the door shouting to someone, and she slipped back into the sitting room. Grace had fallen asleep. Marcia fumbled in her purse for her wallet and slipped two ten rand notes, all she had, under the bottles of medicine where Thandi would be sure to find them.

Even Marcia's warning glance and finger raised to her lips could not stop Sarah's outburst as she let herself into the kitchen door.

"Mamma Ngubane, the children are going wild! I couldn't find Richard — he's gone up the road with the others to watch the fires they started."

Grace woke up with a start. "What fires, Sarah? What are they doing?"

"I didn't see, but Miriam says Richard and his friends heard the school children are marching through Soweto singing and shouting. They are throwing stones and have started a fire at the township office."

Marcia's hand flew to her mouth as she cried out, "Oh no!"

Grace looked over at her with concern. "You'd better hurry and go home, *nkosikazi*. This is not a good time for a white woman to be in Soweto. Go quickly before they get this far."

For a second Marcia couldn't move. She was sure she was having a nightmare; in a moment she would wake up and find herself in her own bedroom. Instead, she heard Sarah crying, "Richard will be hurt, I just know it. The police will stop them and they'll get hurt!" And she threw her apron over her head in a gesture of grief.

Grace remonstrated, "Now Sarah, don't get so upset. Richard is a smart boy. He'll come back if he thinks there's any danger. You go on home — "

"But you can't stay here alone, Grace," Marcia broke in. "You need someone here until Thandi gets home. Even as she said it, she realized Thandi might have difficulty getting home if there was trouble on the streets."

"I'll be all right." Grace smiled weakly. "Sarah can send Miriam over. She's a good girl and she can stay with me until Thandi comes."

Sarah sniffed and wiped her eyes with her apron. "*Yebo*, Mamma Ngubane. Miriam can stay with you. And," she added for Marcia's benefit, "I'll send some of my coal with her so she can build you a fire."

As the door closed behind her, Grace turned to Marcia. "You must go, *nkosikazi*," she said. Once more that look of concern and forgiveness held them for a moment before she whispered in Zulu, "*Nkosi ubusise [God bless you.]*"

Marcia took her hand, her heart flooded with concern and gratitude. "Thank you, Mamma Ngubane. you'll never know what you've done for me today. Good-bye."

Marcia shut the door behind her and stood for a moment on the stoop, filling her lungs with the acrid, smoke-filled air. There was an almost uncanny silence around her; the street was empty of cars and people. Even the ever-present children had disappeared.

Suddenly she heard a roar break out in the distance. It sounded faint and far away, but even from here she recognized it as the sound of a mob whose pent-up anger and frustration had exploded. Intuitively Marcia knew she had to get out of Soweto in a hurry—before that angry mob caught up with her.

SEVENTEEN
The Rescue

As she drove, Marcia wound her way past the land-marks she had so carefully noted on her first trip to Soweto weeks ago. It seemed her best bet was to leave the short way, out through Dobsonville as Geoff had directed her before, rather than take her chances driving back through the township.

"Just don't let me get lost now," she breathed, as she turned at the dry cleaner. Gratefully she recognized the main road ahead. There were more people on the streets now, and she reached over to push down the locks on the doors. She could sense the hostility in the looks people directed her way—so different from the time she was here before.

Suddenly a stone bounced against the side of her car. The youngster who had thrown it dashed around the corner of a house, but she pretended not to notice. She gunned the car forward, moving as fast as possible on the rutted dirt roads.

Her heart sank as she realized she was coming out on the main road at a traffic circle — an insane device designed to slow traffic that was all going in the same direction and allow each vehicle to peel out of the circle at its chosen point of departure. As she eased the Escort into the now heavily trafficked interchange, Marcia felt she was pulling into a trap.

She couldn't pass or hurry. She felt as obvious as an elephant in a flower shop, and could see several young blacks standing on the curb, pointing at her derisively.

Suddenly a van barreled out of one of the entrances into the traffic circle. The car in front of Marcia could not brake fast enough to avoid hitting the van broadside. Marcia frantically swerved to keep from running into him, and her car careened up on the curb. She screamed and slammed on her brakes. But in that instant her front wheel struck a cyclist riding alongside the curb. Horrified, she saw the rider fly into the air as if in slow motion. The bike flipped over and the rider landed, face-down, on the gravel path.

Her instinct was to jump out to help. But as she reached for the handle, a man, his face contorted with hatred, leered through the window, shaking his clenched fist at her.

In a moment, Marcia was surrounded by a crowd screaming angrily and pounding on her car with their hands. Frantically, she shifted into reverse, glancing in the rearview mirror to see if she could back off the curb to get away. The car jerked back a foot and stalled as the mob began rocking it back and forth.

Marcia's hand shook uncontrollably as she put the gear into neutral and tried to start the car again. "I've got to get out of here," she cried as the engine turned over. "O Lord, please help me get away!"

But there was nowhere to go. The van and car in front of her had bottled up the intersection, both too damaged to move on their own power. Vehicles and people poured into the circle until it was a solid mass. As her car tipped dangerously from one side to the other, Marcia screamed "Stop it! Stop it!" She was sure it soon would go over on its side.

At that moment a rock crashed through the windshield, grazing Marcia's cheek. The shatter-proof glass crazed into thousands of cracks and fissures, but only one sharp shard, broken away by the rock, flew into the car and stuck into her arm.

For a moment Marcia stared unbelievingly at the splinter as bright red blood began coursing down her dress. Ironically, she had forgotten to put Band-Aids on her shopping list, as Pieter had reminded her to do.

To Marcia's numbed mind, the shouting seemed far away now. For a second she thought she was having a nightmare. But then another rock flew through the side window, striking her on the side of the head. She realized she was on the verge of losing consciousness, and threw herself down on the front seat, covering her head with her arms for protection. "Help me. O Lord, help me," she prayed.

A cheer came from the crowd, and the next instant a bottle flew against the windshield. The aim was perfect; it broke on impact, splashing its contents through the gaping hole and into the car.

The pungent smell of gasoline was everywhere. Before Marcia could comprehend what was happening, a stone wrapped in a burning cloth flew through the broken window. Instantly flames shot up inside the car as the gasoline ignited.

Frantically Marcia used her handbag to beat out the flames on her skirt. Screaming in terror, she jerked her legs up from the floor where the fire was burning fiercely. Long tongues of flames reached up to the lamb's-wool seat cover and suddenly the entire driver's side was blazing.

Terrified, Marcia screamed again as the flames engulfed her skirt. She felt a searing pain tear at her legs. The rancid smoke burned her eyes and throat, and she began coughing uncontrollably. She knew her only hope was to get out of this blazing trap, even if it meant exposing herself to the frenzied mob outside.

Marcia pushed open the front door and felt rough hands pulling her from the inferno. She collapsed to the ground. Someone threw a heavy coat over her as she lay there, and incredibly she heard a man's voice shouting at the crowd, "Get back! Get back! She needs air."

But the angry crowd had tasted blood, and there was no reasoning with them. Marcia felt a blow on her back as something sharp struck her. The voice once more entreated, "Leave her alone! This isn't going to solve anything."

Suddenly other voices began yelling, "Get back, the car's going to explode!" The roar of the crackling flames, which now totally engulfed the Escort, could be heard above the shouts and screams. People began running in every direction, pushing and shoving to get as far away from the inferno as they could.

Once again strong hands grabbed Marcia, and she was pulled to her feet as a man wrapped a coat around her head and shoulders. By now Marcia was shaking uncontrollably. She could barely lift her feet as the man pulled her along.

"Hurry, madam," he urged in her ear. "The petrol tank will—"

Suddenly a deafening explosion rent the air, sending pieces of debris everywhere. A piece of metal struck a young boy scurrying away in front of her, and Marcia saw him pitch forward, blood pouring from a wound on his head. Shouts of pain gave evidence that others had met the same fate. A girl with her clothes ablaze ran screaming down the street, somehow evading the hands that reached out to catch her and put out the flames.

Marcia stumbled and would have fallen, but her companion supported her with his strong arms. "Come with me, madam. I think I can get you to safety before this mob gathers again. But keep your arms and face covered with the coat as much as possible."

By now the pain in her legs was unbearable.

Glancing down as she stumbled along beside her protector, Marcia saw that the skin on her legs was peeling off in shreds. Her skirt was burned black and hung in tatters around her body, or sticking in places to her seared flesh.

A moan escaped her lips. "I . . . I can't go any further."

"Just a little way, madam, my house is around the corner."

After what seemed like ages, her rescuer pushed open a gate and half-pulled, half-lifted her up a walk and through the front door.

"Themba, come. We need your help," the man called as he led Marcia over to a couch similar to the one in Grace's home. "Lie down here, madam, until we can decide what to do with you."

Through her pain and nausea, Marcia opened her eyes to examine her rescuer as he disappeared into the kitchen to find his wife. His neat business suit was smudged and dirty from pulling her from the fire. His balding head was fringed with gray, and he carried himself erect like a soldier.

In a moment he returned with a woman who was half a head taller than he. Her broad face registered consternation when she saw Marcia. "Hau, hau, Malchus, what have you done bringing a white woman here on a day like today? Don't you know they are going mad out there on the streets?"

"Yes, indeed I know, Themba. They almost killed this woman. They set fire to her car, and when I pulled her out to try to extinguish her burning clothes, they started throwing things at her."

Marcia could hear their voices, but it was as
though they were coming from somewhere in the
a far distance. Still, even in her pain, she wondered
at their use of polished English.

"What is happening to us, Malchus? We're no
better than they are." Themba asked as she came
over to the couch to look down at Marcia.

"She's shaking all over, Malchus. Bring me
some blankets from the bedroom."

But when Themba tried to pick up the coat
which Malchus had thrown over Marcia's legs,
Marcia screamed with pain. Themba shook her
head in concern. "You must get her to a hospital,
Malchus. She's been badly burned. Can you call a
taxi?"

"I don't think taxi drivers would take a chance
carrying a white woman today. Besides they're not
allowed to carry European passengers."

"But," Themba protested, "this is an
emergency!"

"It doesn't matter. I don't think there is a driver
who would do it. If he was stopped by other passengers or by a mob, he might lose his taxi — and
even his life."

"But what can we do? She can't stay here. She
could die! From the way some of those cuts on her
face and arm are bleeding, they must be deep.
Those burns look terrible, Malchus. I don't like
the way she's breathing. If she dies here . . ."
Themba clapped her hands over her mouth as the
horror of the possibility came over her.

"I'll go and get my brother's van. I can put her in
the back of that and no one will see her. Then

when it gets dark, I'll drive into Johannesburg and take her to the General Hospital."

"He'll never let you borrow his van to take a white woman to the hospital. He and his political friends were probably the ones throwing the rocks at her this afternoon."

"I won't tell him what I want it for. If I offer to rent it, he'll be willing enough to let me use it. I only hope he's home and not off somewhere." He looked down at Marcia whose face looked almost as white as the pillow on which she lay. "Here, help me put these extra blankets on top of the coat so she can keep warm. Careful now, don't bump her. She seems to be in a lot of pain. I'll be back with the van as soon as I can."

The last thing Marcia heard was her rescuer's insistent command to his wife: "Themba, lock the door behind me — and don't let anyone in!"

EIGHTEEN
The Escape

Darkness was falling by the time Marcia heard a car drive up and a door slam. Themba got up from the chair where she had been keeping vigil and furtively pulled back the drapes which she shut as soon as Malchus left.

The two women had spoken little. Marcia drifted in and out of consciousness, the pain in her legs and arms stabbing at her until she could no longer hold back the moan in her throat. She dared not move even her hands, which were hot and sticky under the rough blankets.

At one point she asked for water, but when Themba tried to lift her head to hold the glass to her lips, Marcia shook her head. She could stand thirst better than being moved.

Themba had switched the light on in the kitchen while she ran the water but turned it off immediately. From the outside the house looked deserted. That's just what Themba intended.

Once a knock on the back door had brought Marcia to full consciousness. She saw Themba jump out of her seat and tiptoe toward the kitchen. But in a few minutes she was back, explaining in a whisper, "They're gone. It was just a neighbor boy, probably looking for our son."

But now as she peered through the crack in the drapes, Themba sounded relieved. "Malchus is here with Mishack's van."

She had the door unlocked even before he knocked. "Did you have any trouble getting the van?"

"He wanted to know where I was going on a day like today. The streets are wild and there are policemen everywhere."

"What did you tell him?" Themba asked anxiously, throwing the bolt behind Malchus.

"I said a neighbor was sick and had to get to Baragwanath, and with all the trouble it was next to impossible to get a taxi. He didn't really want to let the van out on the streets today, but when I said this neighbor was able to pay for any damages, he relented."

Malchus glanced inquiringly over at Marcia. In the darkness he could barely see her features. "How is she?"

"The same I think," Themba responded. "She moans once in a while. I don't know how you're going to get her into the van. She didn't even want to move when I offered her some water."

"You don't think she can walk with our help?" He bent over Marcia, then turned back to Themba. "Switch the light on. With the van outside, people know there's someone here anyway. I've got to see what the situation is with this woman."

Marcia opened her eyes a crack. Malchus was peering down at her, consternation written all over his round, kindly face. He shook his head in dismay. "Terrible, terrible," he muttered. "Look Themba, she seems to have stopped bleeding from those cuts on her forehead, but her eyes are swollen almost shut. She must've fallen into the dirt when she was pulled out of the car. There's dirt and soot rubbed into those cuts. Those burns on her forehead are blistering."

"But the burns on her legs and arms are far worse," Themba said with concern. "I'm worried, Malchus. I don't like the way she's breathing."

Malchus turned back to Marcia and called gently, "Madam, madam, can you hear me?"

Almost imperceptibly Marcia nodded her head.

"Madam, I have the van here to take you to the hospital. Do you think you can walk if we help you?"

For a moment there was no response. Then Marcia began licking her lips, trying to form the words.

But Malchus stopped her, saying, "Just move your head, yes or no."

After a few more seconds, Marcia slowly shook her head. But even that effort was too much, and tears from her weakness and pain slid out beneath her lids.

Malchus looked perplexed. "How will we get her out of here without help?"

"I have an idea," Themba said. "She's lying on top of a quilt. If we pick up the sides and fold them over her, we can each grab two corners and carry her in a sling. That way we won't have to remove the other blankets either, and the quilt will help keep her warm."

With their plan decided on, Malchus went out to move the van closer to the back door. He was thankful for the winter darkness that had fallen in the past hour. And he was thankful that, on these crisp winter nights, few people hung around outside any longer than they had to. Even the noise of the mob had died down in the last hour. With luck, none of their neighbors would see what they were doing.

Soon Marcia felt herself being lifted off the bed and carried out of the house into the crisp high veld air. As waves of pain poured over her, she felt herself drifting into oblivion. Mercifully, she lost consciousness for a few minutes — long enough for Themba and Malchus to lift her onto the rear seat of the van.

Then she felt the van moving backwards out of the driveway. Suddenly Malchus put on his brakes as Themba shouted and came running up to the window.

"Here, Malchus, you almost forgot her bag. It was lying on the floor."

Malchus reached for the handbag and placed it on the seat beside him. "You sure you won't come along, Themba?"

"No, I'll start cooking so you'll have something to eat when you get home. And Malchus," she reached into the window and grabbed his arm, "you'll be careful, won't you? Do you have your pass? With so many police on the streets tonight, you don't want to be caught without it."

Malchus gave her a reassuring smile and patted his chest. "It's right here in my inside pocket. I don't think the police will bother me tonight. They're too busy rounding up the young people who were in that mob this afternoon. I'll be back in an hour or two. Don't worry, hear?"

He turned to look at Marcia, lying at the rear of the van, totally covered by the blankets and quilts they'd wrapped her in. "I'll try to drive as carefully as I can, madam, but these roads in Soweto are pretty rough. It won't be long before I'll have you at the hospital."

As he'd predicted, the ride was rough and Marcia could feel every twist and turn as it shuddered through her body. But, for some reason, a strange peace poured over her. She felt as if she were outside herself looking down on her battered body being carried along the dark streets of Soweto. There she was, in the middle of an emotional powder keg, in the back of a strange black man's car, burned and injured and half-conscious — but not afraid or angry. She felt surrounded by God's love, assured that nothing would happen to her outside of his will. She didn't even feel anger toward the young people who had injured her. Those kids were just so angry and frustrated they had to take it out on someone; she just happened to be the one to come along.

Then came a thought that caused her some concern: How would she ever be able to explain to Pieter why she had felt the need to come out here in the first place? Would he ever understand?

As she drifted between pain and unconsciousness, the words of a Bible verse kept coming back to her: "Peace I leave with you. . . . Don't let your hearts be troubled . . . and don't be afraid . . . don't be afraid . . . don't be afraid."

Suddenly she felt the van slowing down to stop. *Thank God*, she thought. *We're finally at the hospital.* But as she opened her eyes, she saw red lights flashing on and off out in the darkness and heard the voice of an officer questioning Malchus.

"Where's your pass?"

"Here it is, sir."

There was silence for a moment as the officer flipped through the pass. She couldn't see him but he was obviously checking the picture on the inside cover with the face before him.

"Is this your van?"

"No sir, it's my brother's."

"Where are the papers?"

"In the dash, sir. Do you want to see them?"

"Yes, hurry up about it." The officer shone his flashlight on the license and insurance discs on the windshield and then back into the cab where Malchus was rifling through some papers he'd pulled out of the dash. The light picked up Marcia's handbag lying on the seat beside Malchus.

"Whose purse is that?"

For a moment Malchus hesitated, then started to explain. But it was a moment too long. The officer barked, "Give it here."

Marcia could hear the fear in Malchus' voice, "The bag belongs . . ."

But the officer wasn't listening. He began pulling things out of the purse. Suddenly he called to his partner. "Andre, come here. This bloke has a European woman's handbag on him. Then he jerked open the door of the van and pulled Malchus out of the seat, shouting, "Where did you steal this bag?"

"I didn't steal —"

Marcia heard the blow of a fist against a face, and Malchus's involuntary cry of pain. She wanted to tell the officer that Malchus had rescued her, but she was too weak to call out. Perhaps if she sat up, they would notice her.

The commotion outside the van had grown as several black policemen gathered around Malchus. She could hear them shouting in an African language.

One of the officers instructed the blacks to handcuff Malchus and book him on suspected car theft and stealing a white woman's purse.

"Put him in the paddy wagon, and call a tow truck for the van. We'll probably find this belongs to some European, too."

Marcia knew she had to make her presence known. With one final effort she threw back the covers and forced herself to sit up. The pain of the effort forced a scream to her lips. The last thing she saw before sinking into oblivion was a policeman's flashlight beaming directly into her eyes.

NINETEEN
The Healing

Why am I so hot? I've got too many blankets on me. Marcia tried to throw the covers off, but she couldn't shift. Her arm was heavy and stiff. She grimaced as pain froze her movements.

"Don't move, Marcia, lie still. You're all right." Pieter's worried voice came out of a far distance. Marcia opened her eyes to see bright sunlight pouring into a strange room. This wasn't her bedroom; this was no place she'd ever been before.

"Pieter, where am I?" She turned her head to see him standing beside her bed. He had dark circles under his eyes, and it looked as though he hadn't shaved for days.

"You're in the hospital, Marci. We've been so worried. I finally sent Ouma and the boys home for some sleep a few hours ago. They were here most of the night. You've been sleeping for the last few hours. Don't you remember when the police brought you in last night?"

Suddenly the nightmare came back to Marcia — the fire, the pain, the ride in the ambulance with sirens screaming, the hours in emergency as the nurses and doctors worked over her burns.

She remembered them calling her name: "Mrs. Steyn, don't go to sleep now. You've got a nasty cut on your forehead. We just want to make sure you're all right." It had seemed like ages before they let her sleep, and now she felt as though she never wanted to wake up. Before she could answer Pieter's question, she drifted off in a drugged sleep again.

Marcia lost track of the hours. Now and again she was aware of Pieter sitting beside her bed when she opened her eyes. Once she noticed the darkness outside the window behind him. Several times she was awakened by nurses who apologized as they took her blood pressure or gave her medications. Sometimes the pain became so excruciating she could feel the scalding tears on her cheeks. Then a nurse would come, and she'd soon be asleep again.

Finally, Marcia became aware of sunlight as she opened her eyes. She saw Pieter standing over her, looking anxious and weary. When he saw she was finally awake, he bent down to kiss her, lightly brushing his lips against hers. "Hi, welcome back," he said as he smiled down at her. "You've been out of it for almost two days. How do you feel now?"

"I'm not sure," Marcia said slowly. "It hurts to move." And then as the memory of that night swept over her again, she tried to blink back the tears that brimmed in her eyes. "Oh, Pieter, it was so awful!"

Pieter gently dabbed her eyes with a tissue. "Don't talk now. Eventually I want to hear everything, but you mustn't wear yourself out. We were just so thankful when the police called to say they'd found you. When they rang the first time, they said they'd identified a burned-out car in Soweto as belonging to us. I was frantic! We didn't know where you were. Since both you and the car were gone, we could only assume you were in it."

His voice faltered for a moment, then he continued. "Then they said there was no sign of a body in the wreckage. The police tried to be encouraging, but they didn't sound very hopeful about finding you alive. Dozens of blacks were killed out in Soweto that night; buildings and cars were burned."

He stroked her cheek gently, as though caressing a precious object. "Of course, I kept hoping that the car had been stolen in town and that you'd appear at the front door saying you'd been forced out into the country and had had to walk home."

"How awful for you and the boys," Marcia whispered. "I'm so sorry to have caused so much worry. But I just had to do it, Pieter. I just had to."

"What did you have to . . . ?" Pieter began, then stopped. "No, you shouldn't wear yourself out talking now. You can tell me the whole story later, when you feel stronger."

"No, I want to tell you, Pieter. I'll feel better if you know what happened. Sit down here next to the bed." She started to reach out her hand and remembered her bandages. "I wish I could hold your hand."

Pieter pulled his chair up to the head of the bed and leaned over so his face was close to hers. "OK, I'll listen. But when you get tired just stop, all right?"

"It goes back a long way, Pieter. Even before I became a Christian." When Pieter looked startled, she paused. "I should have told you weeks ago about my experience as a true, new Christian. I've been going to that Bible study at Ruth's, and I began to realize that we've been fooling ourselves to think that because we're 'good' people — law abiding and members of a church — that we're Christians. There's so much more to it than that, Pieter."

For a moment she looked into his eyes to see if he understood. "Being a Christian meant making Jesus Christ the Lord of my life, letting him set my values and direct my actions. Once I began trusting him and using the Bible as the guide for my life, I began to see so many things differently. But I don't think I really understood Christ's forgiveness until I met Grace."

"Who's Grace?" Pieter interrupted.

"Grace is Jacob's mother. She showed me how a true Christian forgives . . . because she has been forgiven. We hurt her and her whole family so much, but I only saw love and forgiveness in her eyes. And I realized that's where we have to start — even in our family."

Pieter looked perplexed. "I don't understand

The Healing

what this has to do with your being hurt, Marcia."

"It has everything to do with it — and especially with why I went out to Soweto yesterday."

"You went to Soweto of your own choice?" Pieter leaned back in his chair and wiped his forehead with the back of his hand.

Marcia nodded. "I was getting so desperate to talk to Geoff and to bring us together again that I got the idea to go down to the African Family Commission where Geoff sometimes works. I thought I might run into him at the office."

Marcia could tell by the set of Pieter's jaw that this wasn't going to be easy. But she knew she had to tell him everything, even about Thandi and Geoff. When she began describing Geoff's declaration of love, Pieter covered his eyes with his hand.

"And so I decided," Marcia doggedly continued, "the only thing that would stop Geoff and Thandi was to tell her mother. Without even planning it consciously, I found myself on the road toward the Baragwanath Hospital."

Pieter listened without a word as she told of her visit with Grace, and the uncommon bond that had sprung up between them.

"Pieter, it's something I can't explain. But suddenly it was as if our hearts were open to each other — as if I understood what she was going through, and she understood my pain. Our families, our people, had been the cause of deep hurt. There was a lot to be forgiven on both sides, but that didn't seem to be an obstacle because God has already forgiven us so much."

Marcia shook her head. "I'm probably not making myself very clear, Pieter. But when the supervisor came around and urged that dying woman to get up and dress so that she could leave the bed for someone else, it seemed the most natural thing in the world for me to offer to take her home. I could no more have left her there than I could have left my own sister."

"So that's how you got out to Soweto on the day of the worst riots in more than fifteen years," responded Pieter thoughtfully. "Weren't you aware the place was blowing up?"

"Not until I was about to leave Grace's house." Marcia went on to describe the scene at the traffic circle. When she told of the mob's part in the fire and explosion, Pieter's face paled and he whispered, "Oh, my God . . . it's a miracle you weren't killed."

"I would have been if it weren't for Malchus."

"You mean that black in whose van the police found you? At least they've got him in custody," he confirmed vehemently. "They found your purse on him."

Marcia looked at Pieter, confused. "But why was he arrested? He risked his life for me. He didn't do anything wrong." She tried to sit up in bed, and an involuntary cry broke from her lips as she disturbed the dressings on her burns.

Pieter realized the excitement was too much for her, and he reached over to press the button for the nurse.

"Don't get upset, Marci. We didn't know. We'll get word to the police about how he helped you. In fact, Dirk and Anna said they would stop by the hospital this afternoon. When Dirk gets here, I'll have him call his good friend, Lt. Van Nie Kerk, the chief of police. Dirk and he are good friends. I'm sure he can arrange his release."

"But you must do something right away, Piet. His wife, Themba, will be so worried. He's been missing for more than two days." Weakened by her ordeal and the pain, Marcia began to cry. "How could they do this to him?"

At that moment the nurse walked into the room in response to Piet's call. He turned to her, his concern reflecting in his voice. "Can't you give her something for the pain? She's going to hurt herself more thrashing around like this." The nurse nodded and prepared the needed medication.

As the injection began taking its effect, Piet stood by Marcia's bed, murmuring soothingly, "It'll be all right, Marci. I'll take care of it. Just close your eyes and get some rest."

Marcia didn't know how long she slept, but when she woke she could see long afternoon shadows playing patterns across the wall. She heard muted voices on the other side of the screen that had been pulled around her bed. Pieter was saying, "So this black pulled her out of the car before it exploded and helped her escape to his house."

"What an awful experience," a woman's voice interjected. Marcia recognized it as Anna's. "How is she now? Is there anything we can do to help?"

"She's been pretty badly burned on her legs and arms and has some deep cuts that required stitches. The doctor says she'll be all right, but she'll be in the hospital for several weeks."

"Can we see her for a few minutes?"

"I think she's still sleeping. The nurse gave her something for pain a couple of hours ago," Pieter replied. "But there is something you can do, Dirk, that would make her feel better."

"You know, Pieter, we'll do anything we can to help," Dirk responded. "It's a terrible thing to have a fine young woman's life threatened by a rampaging black mob. She should never have gone out to Soweto, of course. Out of the goodness and compassion of her heart, she risked her life to help this black woman, and look what it got her."

Dirk's voice took on the tone of a politician. Marcia could almost hear his next campaign speech, extolling the virtues of white womankind and the way they cared for their servants and their servants' families.

"Marcia's upset that the man who rescued her has been arrested," Piet went on to explain. "Is there some way you can contact Van Nie Kerk and explain the situation to him?"

"You want me to get this black released? No, man, you're asking the impossible. Don't you know who he is?"

"I just know his name is Malchus," responded Pieter.

"Ya, Malchus Kunene. His brother Mishak has a dossier at police headquarters as thick as a Bible. This Mishak is a member of the banned Pan-African Congress. He's been trained by the communists when he was out of the country. He's an agitator. We have reason to believe he was involved in planning the riots."

"Why is he still running loose?"

"The CID has been watching him to trace his contacts. They're about ready to pull him in. We didn't have anything on his brother Malchus so far. But you can be sure he wasn't just an innocent by-stander yesterday!"

"But . . . but according to Marcia," Pieter floun-dered, "he saved her life. That doesn't sound like he was involved, does it?"

"Maybe he was afraid things were going too far, who knows? Let the courts decide. I'm not getting my name involved in defending a Kunene." Dirk's voice grew stern as he added, "And you'd better not either, Pieter. It's bad enough Marcia foolishly went out there. But we can't afford to give the op-position opportunities to accuse us of being soft and sentimental — especially with the riots break-ing out as they did. We're too close to the elec-tions."

Marcia wanted to call out to Pieter, to let him know she'd heard everything. But she was too weak to face Dirk now. She heard their voices growing fainter as Dirk and Anna began to leave. Dirk must have turned back into the room, for Marcia could hear him clearly as he said, "Pieter, don't let Marcia tell her story to the police until I get back to you. This is an unfortunate incident, but if we play it smart, it can be to our advantage. And it might be the right time to pull Kunene's brother in to prove we know what's going on out there."

Marcia drifted off into a troubled sleep. When she opened her eyes, night had fallen and the room was dark except for a light above the empty bed beside her. Pieter sprawled in an armchair in the corner, his head tipped to one side against the wall. The light cast heavy shadows on his face, making it look drawn and thin. *Poor Pieter*, thought Marcia as she silently observed his body twitch in sleep. *He's exhausted after the worry and sleepless nights. The past months have been hard on him — the pressures of the campaign and the pain of Geoff's rebellion. Now I've put him between a rock and a hard place again. Dirk certainly sounded as though he meant business about keeping my story about Malchus' part in my rescue undercover.*

She had a vision of Themba standing in the driveway as Malchus pulled out. She remembered how worried she had been about his going into the city on a night like that — how she had checked on his pass to make sure he wouldn't be caught without it. Marcia wondered if Themba had learned of Malchus's arrest. Or was she listening for every footstep in the night as Grace had listened for Jacob's?

Someone's got to let that poor woman know her husband isn't lying unidentified in the morgue, she thought. Then she realized his real situation wasn't much better. There was no way of knowing how long he would rot in the cells before he came to trial. Some comprehension of the real meaning of the 180-day detention law began to dawn on her. Malchus could be kept for six months without anyone knowing where he was or why he was being held.

That was another one of Geoff's gripes. "No government should be able to detain a person without recourse to a lawyer or without knowing what the charges against him are," he had asserted. But because she hadn't really understood, or cared, Marcia had just attributed his agitation to the political atmosphere at the university. It hadn't been anything to be taken seriously.

Suddenly Pieter's head fell to one side, and he sat up with a jerk to keep from falling. When he saw Marcia's eyes on him, he came over to the bed. "Hi . . . how are you feeling? You slept right through dinner. Do you want something to eat?"

Marcia shook her head.

"Pieter," she started tentatively, "I heard you talking with Dirk and Anna this afternoon. Do you think he'll change his mind?"

"About what?"

"About calling Lt. Van Nie Kerk and giving him the true story about Malchus. It's not right to keep him in prison for weeks or even months when he helped save my life."

"Now don't you worry about it, Marci. There are legal channels to follow. I'm sure things will work out for this Malchus. It's you I'm worried about now. You've had a terrible shock and you need to concentrate all your energies on getting well."

Pieter seemed relieved when a young nurse came in to take Marcia's temperature and blood pressure. When she left, Marcia suggested that he go home.

"You look so tired after sitting here with me night and day. I'll be all right. I'm getting the best of care."

"Perhaps you're right. I told Dirk I probably wouldn't be in the office tomorrow. I'll come back and bring Ouma. I know the boys want to come to see you after school, too." He bent to kiss her tenderly. "I'm so thankful nothing worse happened to you. When they brought the news of the burned-out car, I couldn't stand the thought that you might be dead. I love you, Marci."

"I love you too, Pieter. And I thank God every day for you and our wonderful family. If only Geoff—"

Suddenly a voice broke into their conversation, "Mother . . . Dad . . . I just heard about this. I came as quickly as I could. Are you all right, Mother?"

They both turned their heads to see Geoff standing in the doorway, not sure of his welcome.

"Oh, Geoff, I'm so glad you came," Marcia cried. "Come here where I can see you."

Geoff's face registered shock and pain as he looked at her bruised and burned face and the thick bandages on her arms and hands. "I read about your accident in the *Star*. It just said you'd been assaulted in Soweto during the riots, but that they had no details until you were strong enough to speak to the police. What happened?" He glanced at Pieter who had moved to the foot of the bed.

"She was almost killed by a mob out in Soweto. They threw a Molotov cocktail through the windshield, but she got out before the car exploded," Pieter explained coldly. "She'd never have been out in that hellhole if it hadn't been for you!"

"Oh, Pieter," Marcia remonstrated, "don't—"

"He's right, Mother," Goeff interrupted, sinking into the chair next to the bed. "So much of this is my fault." He choked back a sob as he leaned his forehead on the pillow next to hers. "I knew you were out at the Ngubanes'. I found that out this afternoon when Thandi came to the Family—"

"Cut it out, Geoff," Pieter interjected. "Can't you see your mother is in no condition to hear any more melodrama."

"No, Piet, let him talk. We . . . all three of us need to talk." Marcia looked at Geoff compassionately. "I told your dad what happened, Geoff. He knows why I went out to Soweto. But you don't."

"Oh yes, I do, Mother." Goeff leaned back in his chair and wiped the moisture from his eyes with the palm of his hand. "I know because Thandi told me all about your visit. She and her mother had a long talk when Thandi finally got home late that night. The busses weren't running, and the streets were a mess; hundreds were stranded in the city. Thandi found out her mother had been released from the hospital and she started for home."

"I was worried about leaving Grace there alone," Marcia interrupted, "but a neighbor promised to send her daughter over until Thandi arrived."

Geoff nodded. "I guess that's who was with her when Thandi got there. Anyway, Grace told her how you took her home from the hospital and how you left money for food on the table.

"But what impressed Thandi the most was the way the two of you understood each other. You both seemed to feel compassion for the other and recognized the pain and suffering the other was experiencing. I guess Grace had never met a white woman like you before, Mother."

Geoff glanced at his father, who was still standing at the foot of the bed, his hands stuffed into his pockets, jangling his coins and keys.

"Dad . . . you don't have to worry about my marrying a black girl and disgracing you."

Looking back at Marcia he explained, "We both knew it really wouldn't work. We're not ready for it here yet. Children of such a marriage would suffer needlessly, and we knew that the stress of leaving home and family could eventually disintegrate the love we have for each other."

Geoff stood up as if to give his words greater force. "That doesn't mean we don't love each other," he said as he looked directly into Pieter's face. "We love each other very much, but there's no future in it. And we would hurt other people we love — like you and Mother — too much. Grace helped Thandi to see this . . . though I think we already knew it."

Geoff sat down again and looked intently into Marcia's face. "Mother, Grace died this morning in Thandi's arms. But last night before she went to sleep, she told Thandi that your faith in God, your forgiveness for what Jacob did to you, and your willingness to treat her as an equal, gave her peace. She prayed for Thandi and me — and for you. She prayed that God would forgive the blacks and whites for what they are doing to each other."

Geoff looked at Pieter, who tightened his lips to keep his chin from quivering. "Dad, Mother showed us there is another way to handle the hurts in this country. I'm not sure how well it will work for everyone, but I'd sure like for us to give it a try."

For a moment there was silence in the room, broken only by the muffled call for a doctor for an emergency out in the hall. Then Geoff slowly stood up and walked over to Pieter. "Can we try to understand each other, Dad, even though we don't always see eye to eye? Can I come home again . . . please?"

Pieter stretched out his arms, and Geoff fell into his father's embrace. Both were weeping unashamedly, and Marcia thought she'd never seen a more beautiful sight. *Thank you, Lord*, she prayed as she saw the two men she loved begin a reconciliation. And she prayed that they would soon repeat this same scene with their heavenly Father, who she knew was longing to forgive them for so much.

After a few moments, Pieter gently released himself from Geoff's embrace and patted him on the shoulder. "You go on and talk with your mother for a few minutes. Then we'll go home. But first I've got to put in a call," he said, glancing at Marcia, "to Lt. Van Nie Kerk."

And, with a smile of pride and hope in her heart, Marcia watched him stride purposefully out of the room.

Other Living Books® Best-sellers

THE ANGEL OF HIS PRESENCE by Grace Livingston Hill. This book captures the romance of John Wentworth Stanley and a beautiful young woman whose influence causes John to reevaluate his well-laid plans for the future. 07-0047 $2.95.

ANSWERS by Josh McDowell and Don Stewart. In a question-and-answer format, the authors tackle sixty-five of the most-asked questions about the Bible, God, Jesus Christ, miracles, other religions, and creation. 07-0021 $3.95.

THE BEST CHRISTMAS PAGEANT EVER by Barbara Robinson. A delightfully wild and funny story about what happens to a Christmas program when the "Horrible Herdman" brothers and sisters are miscast in the roles of the biblical Christmas story characters. 07-0137 $2.50.

BUILDING YOUR SELF-IMAGE by Josh McDowell. Here are practical answers to help you overcome your fears, anxieties, and lack of self-confidence. Learn how God's higher image of who you are can take root in your heart and mind. 07-1395 $3.95.

THE CHILD WITHIN by Mari Hanes. The author shares insights she gained from God's Word during her own pregnancy. She identifies areas of stress, offers concrete data about the birth process, and points to God's sure promises that he will "gently lead those that are with young." 07-0219 $2.95.

COME BEFORE WINTER AND SHARE MY HOPE by Charles R. Swindoll. A collection of brief vignettes offering hope and the assurance that adversity and despair are temporary setbacks we can overcome! 07-0477 $5.95.

DARE TO DISCIPLINE by James Dobson. A straightforward, plainly written discussion about building and maintaining parent/child relationships based upon love, respect, authority, and ultimate loyalty to God. 07-0522 $3.50.

DAVID AND BATHSHEBA by Roberta Kells Dorr. This novel combines solid biblical and historical research with suspenseful storytelling about men and women locked in the eternal struggle for power, governed by appetites they wrestle to control. 07-0618 $4.95.

FOR MEN ONLY edited by J. Allan Petersen. This book deals with topics of concern to every man: the business world, marriage, fathering, spiritual goals, and problems of living as a Christian in a secular world. 07-0892 $3.95.

FOR WOMEN ONLY by Evelyn and J. Allan Petersen. Balanced, entertaining, diversified treatment of all the aspects of womanhood. 07-0897 $4.95.

400 WAYS TO SAY I LOVE YOU by Alice Chapin. Perhaps the flame of love has almost died in your marriage. Maybe you have a good marriage that just needs a little "spark." Here is a book especially for the woman who wants to rekindle the flame of romance in her marriage; who wants creative, practical, useful ideas to show the man in her life that she cares. 07-0919 $2.95.

Other Living Books® Best-sellers

GIVERS, TAKERS, AND OTHER KINDS OF LOVERS by Josh McDowell and Paul Lewis. This book bypasses vague generalities about love and sex and gets right to the basic questions: Whatever happened to sexual freedom? What's true love like? Do men respond differently than women? If you're looking for straight answers about God's plan for love and sexuality, this book was written for you. 07-1031 $2.95.

HINDS' FEET ON HIGH PLACES by Hannah Hurnard. A classic allegory of a journey toward faith that has sold more than a million copies! 07-1429 $3.95.

HOW TO BE HAPPY THOUGH MARRIED by Tim LaHaye. One of America's most successful marriage counselors gives practical, proven advice for marital happiness. 07-1499 $3.50.

JOHN, SON OF THUNDER by Ellen Gunderson Traylor. In this saga of adventure, romance, and discovery, travel with John—the disciple whom Jesus loved—down desert paths, through the courts of the Holy City, to the foot of the cross. Journey with him from his luxury as a privileged son of Israel to the bitter hardship of his exile on Patmos. 07-1903 $4.95.

LIFE IS TREMENDOUS! by Charlie "Tremendous" Jones. Believing that enthusiasm makes the difference, Jones shows how anyone can be happy, involved, relevant, productive, healthy, and secure in the midst of a high-pressure, commercialized society. 07-2184 $2.95.

LOOKING FOR LOVE IN ALL THE WRONG PLACES by Joe White. Using wisdom gained from many talks with young people, White steers teens in the right direction to find love and fulfillment in a personal relationship with God. 07-3825 $3.95.

LORD, COULD YOU HURRY A LITTLE? by Ruth Harms Calkin. These prayer-poems from the heart of a godly woman trace the inner workings of the heart, following the rhythms of the day and the seasons of the year with expectation and love. 07-3816 $2.95.

LORD, I KEEP RUNNING BACK TO YOU by Ruth Harms Calkin. In prayer-poems tinged with wonder, joy, humanness, and questioning, the author speaks for all of us who are groping and learning together what it means to be God's child. 07-3819 $3.50.

MORE THAN A CARPENTER by Josh McDowell. A hard-hitting book for people who are skeptical about Jesus' deity, his resurrection, and his claims on their lives. 07-4552 $2.95.

MOUNTAINS OF SPICES by Hannah Hurnard. Here is an allegory comparing the nine spices mentioned in the Song of Solomon to the nine fruits of the Spirit. A story of the glory of surrender by the author of *HINDS' FEET ON HIGH PLACES*. 07-4611 $3.95.

NOW IS YOUR TIME TO WIN by Dave Dean. In this true-life story, Dean shares how he locked into seven principles that enabled him to bounce back from failure to success. Read about successful men and women—from sports and entertainment celebrities to the ordinary people next door—and discover how you too can bounce back from failure to success! 07-4727 $2.95.

Other Living Books® Best-sellers

THE POSITIVE POWER OF JESUS CHRIST by Norman Vincent Peale. All his life the author has been leading men and women to Jesus Christ. In this book he tells of his boyhood encounters with Jesus and of his spiritual growth as he attended seminary and began his world-renowned ministry. 07-4914 $4.50.

REASONS by Josh McDowell and Don Stewart. In a convenient question-and-answer format, the authors address many of the commonly asked questions about the Bible and evolution. 07-5287 $3.95.

ROCK by Bob Larson. A well-researched and penetrating look at today's rock music and rock performers, their lyrics, and their life-styles. 07-5686 $3.50.

THE STORY FROM THE BOOK. The full sweep of *The Book*'s content in abridged, chronological form, giving the reader the "big picture" of the Bible. 07-6677 $4.95.

SUCCESS: THE GLENN BLAND METHOD by Glenn Bland. The author shows how to set goals and make plans that really work. His ingredients of success include spiritual, financial, educational, and recreational balances. 07-6689 $3.50.

TELL ME AGAIN, LORD, I FORGET by Ruth Harms Calkin. You will easily identify with the author in this collection of prayer-poems about the challenges, peaks, and quiet moments of each day. 07-6990 $3.50.

THROUGH GATES OF SPLENDOR by Elisabeth Elliot. This unforgettable story of five men who braved the Auca Indians has become one of the most famous missionary books of all times. 07-7151 $3.95.

WAY BACK IN THE HILLS by James C. Hefley. The story of Hefley's colorful childhood in the Ozarks makes reflective reading for those who like a nostalgic journey into the past. 07-7821 $4.50.

WHAT WIVES WISH THEIR HUSBANDS KNEW ABOUT WOMEN by James Dobson. The best-selling author of *DARE TO DISCIPLINE* and *THE STRONG-WILLED CHILD* brings us this vital book that speaks to the unique emotional needs and aspirations of today's woman. An immensely practical, interesting guide. 07-7896 $3.50.